Swept Away

Swept Away

Anne Dale
FGA, PG, GG

ISBN 978-0-692-45372-8

Printed and bound in the United States of America

Library of Congress info available upon request

www.annedale.com

Dedicated to
The Patroness of Louisiana
"Our Lady of Prompt Succor"

Contents

Preface

The American Dream lives in each of our hearts. It is not always about money or fame, but in truth, it is the pursuit of happiness. Our success is gauged by how well we persevere toward our goals, and it is when we achieve our goals that we come to know that it is not an end, but a beginning to even more.

No matter our age, our hearts remain a child of God with desires and dreams governed by Him. God's plan and purpose for each person, regardless of circumstance, extends beyond the physical world, from the immeasurable vast universe to the tiny, complex atom. Life may not always go according to our plan, but if we live and thrive with faith, God will make a new path for us, every step of the way.

As you read this book, much like the journey of life, I hope you laugh, cry, and reflect, but most of all become inspired to live life from the inside out. I wish you strength to live true to yourself and your ambitions.

This book is based on true stories from memories and recollections. To protect the privacy of some individuals, their names have been changed.

Acknowledgments

I give my deepest thanks to my family for their patience, support, and encouragement. I give my gratitude to my best friend, business partner and husband of more than thirty years, Michael Dale. I thank my children, Stephen, Paul, and Grace, whom I am proud of for embracing the higher values of God, family, and country as they journey through life. I am grateful for the support and assistance of family and friends who never grew discouraged or tired of me in the time it took to complete this book while balancing work and family: Catherine Schroeder, Amy Minnick, Julia Juge, Ina Hecker, Cheryl Farris, Dawn Uratta, Rachel Jones, and Lauren Gast. I also thank those who embody inspirational perseverance such as Mr. Lawrence Schlaudecker. Finally, but most importantly, I thank God.

Swept Away

CHAPTER 1
Changing Winds
The Storms of Life

Aftermath of Hurricane Katrina, 2005

Te storms of life can take us by surprise, blinding us with fear and uncertainty, darkening our dreams—but only if we let them.

Life's storms bring about changing winds, and for me one in particular I recall...

August 29, 2005: claps of thunder abruptly woke me from a deep sleep at five o'clock in the morning. Although the room was dark, I could hear the wind begin to change. I knew the unexpected—with all of its effects—was now on its way. I would have to embrace all that lay beyond my control, along with the decisions I had made. Feeling rather vulnerable, I took a slow, deep breath and began praying, "Our Father ..." Suddenly John 3:8 entered my mind: " The wind blows where it wills, and you can hear the sound it makes, but you do not know where it comes from or where it goes: so it is with everyone who is born of the Spirit."

I

Hurricane Katrina would challenge the human spirit and bring out the best and worst in many people. The day's events would make history, changing America's view on the role of government as well as the nation's procedures and policies on preparedness in the face of catastrophes. The effects of that day's storm—initially thought to last for just hours—went on for months, and for many it changed the course of their lives forever. Even Hollywood developed entertaining spins based on these events, from thrill-seeking zombie movies to dramas such as *The Curious Case of Benjamin Buttons, The Walking Dead*, and *Treme*.

As the thunder rumbled, I tossed in bed. Filled with anticipation, I decided to get up and put on a pot of coffee. As I made my way to the kitchen, I curiously peered out a window, but only the darkness was visible. The absence of light only heightened my sense of hearing, causing me to listen intently to the strengthening rain and winds. My mind wandered about. Trying not to be frightened, I closed my eyes and welcomed the wind gusts to jog a pleasant memory, a memory of many years ago, a memory of Lady Liberty.

I was seventeen years old. It was a crisp fall day. The Atlantic winds were blowing my hair about, stinging my face. I was on the Staten Island Ferry sailing toward the Statue of Liberty. As I got closer, her size and grandeur impressed me greatly. Back in 1979, anyone who was willing and able could climb up into her crown, and I eagerly welcomed the challenge. Anxiously waiting in line, I imagined how high in the sky I would actually be and what I would see once I reached the top. But as I heard other people in line talk about her height, fear tiptoed into my mind. I wondered if in the high altitude I would feel the effects of the wind blowing. I asked the park ranger, "Does the statue sway in the wind?"

Leaning in toward me he said, "The statue can sway up to three inches and her torch as much as five inches in a fifty-mile-an-hour wind, but don't worry. Lady Liberty will never bend or fall. She always remains stable."

Wanting to be at ease, I let my excitement outweigh those concerns. The line moved at a snail's pace up a tight, circular stairwell. Looking up, all I could see was the derriere of the person in front of me. While impatiently waiting, I tried to feel if the statue swayed. Finally, an agonizing hour later, I made it to the top. I was now able to see what she observes day after day. Breathing deeply, I sighed joyfully at the magnificent view. I felt inspired to make a wish as I made a point to look out each of the twenty-five windows in her crown. I wished to see the world as she did. I wished for the chance of opportunities—opportunities that would allow all of my dreams to come true, even if I didn't know what they were yet.

That day as I read the words of a sonnet by Emma Lazarus etched in Lady Liberty's base, I took pride in my country, for she is generous, charitable, and magnificent.

> *Give me your tired, your poor,*
> *Your huddled masses yearning to breathe free.*
> *The wretched refuse of your teeming shore.*
> *Send these, the homeless, tempest-tost to me.*
> *I lift my lamp beside the golden door!*

Suddenly, the coffee pot sounded off with a beep, the brewing finished, and my golden memory left me. Reflectively, I sat sipping my coffee at the kitchen table, reviewing the decisions and preparations made in the past forty-eight hours, and hoping for the best. We were at our family jewelry store when we first received news of a mandatory evacuation. I walked outside to the front of the store to see how others were responding. I felt the sweltering heat of a typical hot, humid Louisiana day. Looking up at the sky, all seemed clear and calm. But when I looked down the street, I saw that this day would be anything but ordinary. The corner gas stations were already crowded with anxious evacuees waiting in long lines. Traffic began to fill the streets with nervous drivers wanting to get out of town. There was an eerie Twilight Zone sensation that began to settle in the air, like being in a scary movie, except it was real.

However, that particular day was supposed to be special, a day of celebration for Mike and me, not a day of chaos. It was our twenty-second wedding anniversary. That evening we planned a romantic sailboat ride on Lake Pontchartrain. I had envisioned sipping wine and watching the sunset, but "her" short notice of arrival changed our plans. Uninvited, she was coming . . . Hurricane Katrina. She would be the big one, the "CAT-FIVE" that everyone feared would one day come.

Due to Katrina's enormity, all of South Louisiana was advised to prepare and take every precaution necessary. Mandatory evacuations were issued throughout Louisiana's coastal parishes, which included certain cities such as New Orleans and Mandeville. Mandeville is where our family jewelry store is located, about one mile from Lake Pontchartrain, which flows into the Gulf of Mexico.

Heeding the calls for evacuation, we began time-consuming preparations. In the unfortunate event of destruction or looting, the store required much security. The precautionary task of packing jewelry, computers, shop equipment, and anything else needed to operate our business in a new location proved daunting.

Soon after, we joined the bumper-to-bumper convoy of traffic and trekked home. Inching very slowly, at ten miles per hour, we listened to the radio, absorbing any information we could get. The slow-moving contra flows, stalled vehicles, gas station closings, and mass exoduses from major U.S. cities was unlike anything in recorded American history.

Normally, the ride from our business to home in rural St. Tammany Parish would take only twenty minutes, but with the traffic, it took us two hours to arrive. To our surprise, as we turned into the driveway of our five-acre home, we saw anxious, evacuated family members who were anticipating our arrival. They were from neighboring cities that would be impacted by Katrina. Nineteen of us gathered together as we watched television broadcasts. Confusing and conflicting reports about the mandatory evacuation in our hometown caused uncertainty as to whether we should leave or stay. Stress weighed us down. We had much to consider—children, family, those who wanted to stay and ride out the storm, taking refuge in our house. The dreadful news continued with reports of gas shortages and no hotel vacancies within hundreds of miles, including neighboring states. There was even more to consider: our family business. Mike and I chose to stay and ride out Katrina. However, we still strategized possible last-minute escape routes.

Some family members decided to leave and head further north to a safer area. Now there were thirteen of us in the house. Because the family was together, the mood at times was festive. But our anticipation and underlying anxiety was put to good use as everyone was helpful in preparing the home for Katrina.

We inventoried canned goods, stored water in jugs, pots, and bathtubs. We washed all dirty clothing in case the electricity was out for a while. We gathered candles, flashlights, batteries, an axe, a hammer, a first-aid kit, and radios. With thoughts of possible tornadoes, we hurriedly searched for loose things in the yard that could be dangerous in strong winds, like bikes, patio furniture, hoses, plants, or any other debris around the property. We boarded and taped up windows to reduce flying glass in the event they were blown out from changes in air pressure. Everyone positioned their cars close to the front of the house, away from trees and in case a quick getaway was necessary.

Sunday morning, August 28th, we spotted a few neighbors driving like bats-out-of-hell through the neighborhood; they had changed their minds and fled. As they sped away, Mike and I turned to face each other. Our eyes met, but no words were exchanged—just a look, a mutual understanding that we both questioned our decision to stay and wondered if we should follow their lead. We reflected on the fact that we were only a few miles outside of the mandatory evacuation boundaries. Our city mayor had requested that the elderly and those with special needs evacuate. We tried to reassure ourselves that we were safe. We still had hope that she, Katrina, would turn away, or that her strength would diminish once she made landfall like other hurricanes in the past. But hours later, she was still heading in our direction, getting closer and stronger.

As we waited for Katrina, the children seemed to draw their energy from the nervous adults. I gathered the seven children together, whose ages ranged from two to sixteen. In an attempt to calm their uncertainty with truth, I told them, "We're having an important meeting. You will hear loud noises from the wind and the rain. You must keep your shoes on at all times, just in case we have to run to the neighbors'."

One of the kids asked, "Why do we have to run to the neighbors?"

"Do you remember the movie *The Wizard of Oz*?"

"Yes," they replied.

Delicately, with as much of a comforting tone as I could muster, I told them, "Well, the wind might blow things off of the house like the roof. But instead of running into the cellar with Auntie Em, we will run with Aunt Anne to the house across the street." I nodded my head with a subtle smile as if to imply there was no need to worry.

As if things were not scary enough in my explanation, I added, "If you hear the sound of a train, run into the bathroom and get in the bathtub." It was the only way I knew to explain the sound of a tornado.

Their eyes filled with wonder, as if it sounded like this safety measure could be an enjoyable game. It was probably a good thing they didn't understand the seriousness of Katrina or what I was trying to convey.

SWEPT AWAY

Bright lights flashing from my kitchen window, followed by loud claps of thunder, brought me back to the present moment. My coffee mug was empty. I needed more cream before a refill. Exhausted, I stared into the refrigerator waiting for the container to notice me when suddenly the house became silent. The electricity went out, and I was blinded by darkness. A storm of life was approaching; Hurricane Katrina was knocking at the front door.

CHAPTER 2
When the Blind Man Knocks
Unforeseen Gifts

Anne at the dinner table, 1968

Trying to find my way around the dark house brought me back to 1969. I was only six years old, and I was helping my mother clean the kitchen after breakfast when we heard an unexpected knock. Curious, I stood by her side as she opened the front door.

There stood a very tall, thin man. Because I was only three feet in height, I had to tilt my head back to get a better look at him. He was balancing several weighty brooms over his shoulder, their bristles pointing upward. He wrapped his arm securely around them while balancing his stance with a walking stick in the other hand. I had never seen anyone like him before. He seemed strange and mysterious to my young eyes. The man asked my mother if she would like to buy a broom.

"How much?" she asked.

"Three dollars," said the man.

Mama told him that she had to go get her purse. She walked away. Silently, I surveyed him with great interest. Level to my eyes was a flicker that demanded most of my attention. It was a ring on his finger that glistened unlike any color I had ever seen in my crayon box. I was mesmerized by the sparkly stone set inside of it. Watching how the ring captured the light made it seem magical, and I wondered what kind of special powers the ring might hold.

As I gazed at the ring, the man said, "Hello."

I froze. I was taught not to talk to strangers. Scared, I said nothing.

He said hello again, and still I said nothing. I noticed he was staring straight into my mama's house. Inquisitively, I swung my head around to catch a glimpse of what he was looking at, but I didn't see anything. I looked back at him, and he was still staring into mama's house. His behavior confirmed that there was some-thing different about him than most people. As mama walked up he tucked his walking stick under his arm and opened the palm of his hand. After mama placed the money in his hand, he gathered it tightly and tucked it away in his corduroy pants pocket. Squatting down very slowly, he slid the weighty brooms off of his shoulder and stood them straight up on the floor of mama's porch. He asked mama which broom she wanted.

"Any one of them will do," she answered.

Brushing them with the passing of his fingertips, he handed her the one with the best bristles. He grunted softly as he lift-ed the bundle back onto his shoulder and cordially thanked my mother for her business. Tapping his walking stick several times on the porch, he turned around and stepped off. As mama closed the door, I quickly ran to the nearest window so I could study him some more.

"Mama, why does he walk like that, tapping that stick?"

"He's blind. He can't see."

"Blind?"

"Yes. He uses his cane to guide his steps when he walks. He makes and sells brooms to earn a living."

"Mama, then tell me why are his eyes open?"

Going about her house chores she answered me. "Well, he can still see people with his mind and his heart."

"Can he see me?"

"Only if you want him to."

"Where does he live?"

"I don't know."

"Mama, where does he make his brooms?"

She tried not to lose her patience with me as I asked many questions. "I don't know. Don't you have some coloring you want to do?"

"Mama, how does he see to sweep?"

"I don't know!"

As a child, I remember trying to walk around the house with my eyes closed like the blind broom man. I wanted to see how long I could go before bumping into something. I couldn't keep from opening my eyes to peek, so I blindfolded myself with a scarf. With the scarf tied tightly over my eyes, I would attempt to eat at the dinner table but would constantly miss my mouth with the fork.

I was so fascinated by the blind broom man; I couldn't wait until he returned. Each time he came to sell his brooms, I wondered about him even more. Sometimes, I would secretly follow him down the street. I watched how skilled he was at balancing all those brooms. With his arms full, he walked on the lopsided, broken sidewalks that hugged the big oak trees which lined our street. I would watch how he never looked to the right or to the left before crossing the street. I watched how he stepped up onto the neighbor's porch without looking down. I counted the times he would knock on their doors, who bought his brooms and who didn't. Sometimes I got close enough to hear what he said to them as he sold his brooms. Each time I looked for the shimmering, magical ring he wore on his finger.

Even though he couldn't see me, I felt he somehow knew I was there.

Years later, he slowed down his walk along those crooked sidewalks. He carried fewer brooms. One day, he knocked at the door and was not wearing his magical ring. That was the first time I gathered up my courage to speak to him.

"Where's your magic ring?" I asked.

A wistful smile worked its way slowly across his face. "I had to sell it for some money."

"Why?"

"It's just how it is in life."

"Will you still have the magical powers to make the brooms?"

Pausing, he realized my childlike implication. Quick on his feet, he replied, "Yes, because I wore it for so long the magic became a part of me."

Somehow, as a child, I got the notion that the "magical" ring gave the blind man the sight to see how to make the brooms and sweep the floors.

It wasn't long until I didn't see the broom man anymore. I never knew his name, his story, or what happened to him. It's interesting how sometimes the people we know the least about can have the biggest effect on us. He was my first teacher of business, and by his example, he taught me. As with every great teacher, they teach more lessons than one. It was because of him I had learned at a young age to see the world a little differently and to hear it in a new way.

Always being someone with a curious nature, I seemed to take notice of people who were different after meeting the blind man. He taught me the importance of seeing within people, especially those with special needs. As I thought about them, I tried to take into account what they experience. As a child, I would imagine what I could or could not do, like tie my shoes with one hand. I would cover my ears to imagine what it would be like if I were deaf. Although they started as a child's game, as I got older my games would weigh a little more seriously upon my heart.

The neighborhood I grew up in had many intriguing adults and a lot of captivating kids. Just a few doors down from my house lived my friend named Maria who was deaf. Even though Maria taught me to communicate by signing the alphabet, we still spoke the same language of adolescent perceptions. Her parents, much like mine, were very protective of their daughter. Maria had huge mirrors on the handlebars of her bike to help her see what she couldn't hear. Permission had to be granted just for her to walk beyond the sidewalk that was in front of her house. During neighborhood parties, we turned up the music real loud so that she could feel the vibrations through the floor, and we would dance. When her older brother picked on her, we laughed together as she told him off in sign language.

One day, I got a glimpse into her world. She invited me to hang out with her friends for an event at her school, a school for the deaf. There I stood in a circle of about ten hearing-impaired kids. Many hands moved quickly, all of them signing at the same time, or so it seemed to me. I couldn't keep up or understand anyone. I felt left out. Feeling different made me wonder if it was more convenient for them not to include me, a similar experience to the one Maria probably encountered every day in a world filled with noise. Maria's patience for being hearing impaired was admirable, and she always maintained a great sense of humor. I was enriched by our friendship.

Down the block was a friend whose uncle had cerebral palsy. Whenever I knocked on her door, her uncle answered in his wheelchair, ready to engage in conversation. But with his speech impairment, it seemed I did most of the talking and he did most of the listening. I was always amazed at how my friend could understand her uncle perfectly in their conversations and wished I could too. Trying to get in on their conversations, I would concentrate, listening carefully to them converse. But it seemed I lacked something in my ability to hear that caused me to remain deaf to certain tones. I could only surmise that their language went beyond what was audible; it was a language of the heart.

Another neighbor named Mrs. Bordelon, who lived in the house across the street from ours, was a recluse, afraid to go outside. I would watch as she fearfully peeked out from behind the faded drapes in the front window of her home. It seemed as if those drapes protected her from the world or from the loud and wild neighborhood kids like me. Curious, I found numerous reasons to knock at her door just to see if she would answer. I wanted her to know it was safe outside and we weren't bad kids; she didn't have to be afraid. She never did answer the door. I never saw any other part of her body except her large eyes. Her face remained hidden behind the drapes that separated our two worlds. Eventually, I lost interest and gave up. But sometime later, one afternoon, an ambulance pulled up to the front of her house. As I saw paramedics enter her home, all I could think about was how she must have never gone to the doctor and how flipped out she must be leaving her safety net, her home. Out of the house she came, strapped to a gurney, rolled away, and still all I could see was her large eyes. That was the last time I ever saw her.

As far as other adults in the neighborhood, we had the alcoholics, the convicted child molester we stayed away from, the wife beater, and the rock-and-roller who played awful, screeching music with his band into the late hours of the night. There was the policeman, the potato chip delivery man, the church lady, the dog lady, and there was Tojo who forever walked the streets of the neighborhood. He looked too old to be hanging out with all the younger kids, but he was harmless. I felt bad when some of the other kids made fun of him. No one ever saw his parents or really knew where he lived, but he was always around. There was the big lady, a mean lady who would not let us turn our bikes around on her empty driveway, the troubled teenager who went to jail, and then there was the house that was haunted. No one seemed to live in it, but every once in a while one of the neighborhood kids would swear they saw someone inside.

I thought everyone grew up in a neighborhood like ours. It wasn't until later in life that I realized otherwise.

As I hit my teens, the neighborhood changed—we were growing up. Periodically, I entertained myself by pondering the question that everyone thinks about in their youth: "What am I going to be when I grow up?" I thought when the time was right the answer would just fall out of the sky and land in my lap. Little did I realize, that question was going to be answered through encounters, opportunities, and people who influenced me, as well as the choices I made.

For my sixteenth birthday my parents surprised me with my first piece of nice jewelry. It was a beautiful ring that held a glistening gemstone. It wasn't exactly like the blind broom man's ring, but it would be, for me, my very own magical ring. Underneath a bright lamp in our living room, I studied its details, entertaining myself by watching the gem flicker as I moved it about. Staring into the ring, I would allow my mind to fill with ambitious ideas of future dreams and possibilities, hoping that somehow the gem would reveal my future. Having my ring made me feel grown up, special, and I welcomed the inner feeling that I had a purpose in life. I believed I was destined for something unique and that an exciting journey awaited me. I couldn't wait to grow up and experience it. I wore my ring every day because it meant that I mattered in this great big world.

A few years later, as a young adult, my path would cross with a woman who had multiple sclerosis. The parallels of this encounter would further intersect with the blind broom man, the magical ring, and the answer to what was I going to be when I grew up—my destiny. I was working in a retail store. The woman with MS would often come to the shop. She was in a motorized wheelchair. She wore a fitted neck and back brace that helped her to sit up. Sadly, her health declined, and she became homebound. She asked me to visit her, and so, with hesitation, I did. I hesitated because my life was very full at the time, but the truth was that I felt so sad for her that it made me feel bad to be around her. I had trouble getting past her disease to see her for who she really was. Much of my energy was focused on how I felt. Wanting to take the high road in life, I agreed, and in my selfishness, I thought she would benefit from my visits. As time went on, I learned more about her circumstance and that our encounters were benefitting me. I was growing as a person.

She lived in an old trailer in a poor area of town. I would visit only to learn more and more about how much she suffered. Each visit just seemed to bring on more sorrow for me. She lay in bed, all ninety pounds of her, hooked to a tube that would feed her intravenously. I would learn that at the age of sixteen she was raped and conceived a child who lives today. She was legally blind and had difficulty breathing. I was at a loss for words and really didn't know what to say to her, especially when she was physically uncomfortable and very down about life. Reluctantly, I dragged myself up the steps to her house, praying for the grace from God to help me say the right things to her. I felt bad when I would leave her, and yet I felt relieved too. It was emotionally heavy and draining. I was just "Anne," not a therapist or a medical aid—such professionals have a calling to help people.

I believed my faith in God to be strong, but one day she would shake my foundation and test me by asking the question I feared I couldn't answer: "Why did God let this happen to me?"

Pausing, I responded, "I don't know . . . I don't have an answer."

In our relationship, we shared not only each other's company, but conversations about faith. In those conversations, she would again seek an answer to the question, "Why did God let this happen to me?"

Each time, I longed to give her some meaningful answer that would make sense to us both. One day while asking me the same question, I hung my head down desperately searching in my faith for truth when suddenly a glimmer of light caught my eye. It was a flicker that came from my ring, the ring I always wore, my special ring, the ring that connected my memories to the blind broom man. Like him, I responded, "It's just how life is."

Words began to roll off my tongue.

"You are very special and possess the magical ability to share your gifts with the world—gifts of the human spirit, exemplifying courage, perseverance, sacrifice, and above all, a great appreciation for life, an appreciation that takes most people their entire life to come to learn."

Somehow I knew it was time to pass on my ring that signified "purpose" to someone who really needed it. I took off the ring and placed it on one of her fingers. I then held her hand in view so that she could see the beauty of the glistening gem. I thanked her.

"You are a rare find of a gem that glistens in the darkness," I told her. "You allow others to use your light so that they can see the world and people with new eyes. Thank you."

Another great teacher in my life, she had taught me to be a better person.

I have come to learn that every person, no matter circumstances, is graced with gifts, big or small, and that every gift matters in our big, complex, yet purposeful universe. Sometimes a gift needs to be discovered, and at times our gifts are revealed through shared encounters with someone or an unexpected opportunity. As a Christian, I refer to them as "God's Course Setters."

Another experience that led me to this belief was a profound dream I had. The dream took place during a time in my life when I was making a significant career decision. In the dream, I was at the height of my career and I was being considered for the opportunity to be a presenter, to recognize someone of a high-ranking, national status. The recipient's award was a beautiful and rare crystal geode. Feeling entitled because of my earned credentials as a gemologist that I should be the person to present, I rattled off a litany of my accomplishments with why "I" should be chosen.

Suddenly, in the dream I was asked by the Wisest, "Tell me Anne, what is your gift and who is it for?"

I awoke pondering the question: if my gifts were for only me, what purpose would they serve?

CHAPTER 3
A Child's Journey
A Desire to Dream

Anne, ready to launch her first rocket ship, 1970

All children dream dreams. They challenge their imagination by making their pretend world as real as possible. Unfortunately, as we grow older, our daily routines and responsibilities cause us to let go of that magical ability to dream. Often when we revisit our childhood, it puts a smile on our face, and we recall who we really are in our adult bodies. By reflecting on our lives, we realize that our God-given gifts were surfacing all along our journey in life.

I was ready to experience and to journey the world by age seven. I grew up in a small, three-bedroom house with four sisters in Kenner, Louisiana. Our street, Kansas, was lined with oak trees on both sides. I also grew up with at least twenty other kids in the neighborhood. There, I would experience my first kiss, my first crush, and my first make-believe wedding. I would learn to toughen up when playing dodgeball with the boys and rejoice when I outran one of them in a race. We picked and ate blackberries, honeysuckles and mirlitons off the fence. We grabbed our buckets and headed to the empty corner lot, collecting and eating pecans that fell to the ground from the aged pecan trees. We played hide-and-seek from one end of the street to the other. We raced go-carts down the back alleys, swung on a rope from the tallest oak tree and found four-leaf clovers. As I lose myself in those memories, I can still smell the St. Augustine grass as I lounged in it barefoot, staring up at the moving clouds above.

For as long as I can remember, my parents allowed me access to only one end of the street and back. Frustrated with my restricted perimeters, I would escape by riding my bike like the wind, daydreaming of my future and thinking about freedom. I dreamed about the day I would ride past the end of the street to see the world that was waiting for me.

Periodically, a glorious occasion would occur, and an opportunity of freedom would bring me beyond those borders to the little convenience store. Such luck came about when my parents had a last-minute grocery need. Feeling empowered on those errands, I would sometimes walk slowly so that I could experience every adventurous step along the way, hoping for something to happen, someone to see or lost treasure to discover. That little corner convenience store was only three blocks away, but to me it was in another world. Every time I visited the little Handy Pack store, I'd walk up and down every checkered-tile aisle, taking note of everything that was there, identifying the new products, and analyzing how the store owner displayed them. Since I studied product pricing too, I hoped and imagined that one day I would be on the television show The Price is Right and win big. I especially studied the candy section—the different colors, sizes, prices, and oh, the smells! I'd daydream that one day when I was a teenager I would be able to work there. I hated having to walk back home carrying an overstuffed grocery bag that blocked my vision because they infringed on my imagination and my ability to observe the outside world of my neighborhood.

Time and again I wished I had money to buy myself some candy because then the walk back home would be worth it. So I did what any kid would have done at my age—I began to barter with my parents, asking for money to buy candy in exchange for the store errand. Learning to barter taught me lessons on creating opportunities. However, having to depend on my parents for candy was not as sweet as I wanted it to be. So I began to think of other ways to earn my own money. I babysat, put on talent shows, cleaned houses, washed cars, washed a neighbor's boat, weeded gardens, and fed dogs while an owner was out of town. I did it all, even hand-painted themed shirts to sell door-to-door in my neighborhood, just like the blind broom man. I was now earning my own money and discovering independence. I now had freedom to buy what I wanted—candy. Mindful of my hard-earned money, I carefully studied every candy before weighing my options —Mary Janes for a penny or chewy Tootsie Rolls.

But as I got a little older, I began to take notice of additional things that kids seem to value. In my neighborhood, I saw kids playing with colorful, beautiful marbles. They guarded and showed off their prized collections. Intrigued, I watched how they played and negotiated with bigger marbles called "boulders." The boulders seemed to have strength and offered greater bartering power. I wanted to have my own marbles and boulders; I wanted to experience and learn the power to negotiate with my peers, especially with the older kids. The cat's eye marbles were my favorite. I was fascinated as to how they got a real cat's eye inside. Until I figured out how, I wouldn't risk losing my cat's eyes in any challenging marble games.

My desire to dream and my curiosity to see and to experience all that could be accomplished within my one-block universe kept me extremely busy. I had big ambitions. One time I was going to earn enough money to buy a horse and keep him in my backyard.

Letting him outside of his limited quarters, I imagined racing him up and down the street of my universe. I daydreamed about how high in the air I would sit on that horse and how I'd enjoy feeling the wind in my face.

I was not the shy kind of kid either; I would dream that I was going to be on TV. I would practice toothpaste commercials in the mirror or rehearse as an actress in a movie with Elvis Presley. I miss those days because never did I doubt my dreams. With the innocence of a child's heart, I really believed anything was possible. The wonderment of the marbles never left me, and to this day, I still have my bag of marbles.

I began a hobby of collecting colorful, shiny objects. The Easy Bake oven helped broaden my horizons as I put it to an interesting use. Instead of making cakes, I melted Mardi Gras beads together in the baking pans, creating vibrant pendants to wear. Designer-conscious, I carefully laid out an assortment of beads that complemented each other in color and shape. I would sit on top of the kitchen counter and peek into the oven, watching the molten design fuse into one big conglomerate. Over and over again, I would create until my mother couldn't take the smell in her house any longer.

As I discovered my creativity, I wanted to make more designs, especially jewelry, to wear or possibly sell—but I was in need of gems. My mother would find me scanning through her collection of jewelry that was neatly arranged in her red, velvet-lined, rosewood jewelry box. She had an assortment of pearls, earrings, broaches, and a bracelet filled with charms that told many stories of her journeys. Knowing her treasures were off limits, as she frequently reminded me, I had to find a source to bring my design ambitions to life. So I searched for the closest thing I had access to—rocks and broken glass. I searched in gravel roads, dirt piles, and underground.

Then, somehow it happened, and I began to have a fascination with rocks and crystals. My interest, along with a sought-after opportunity, began to create a destiny, and I was hooked. I studied everything from the tiniest pebbles to broken pieces of glass that I would find on my street curbs. I would dig in my parents' yard, hoping to find the great kahuna, the rock that has yet to be discovered by mankind. My parents were not too pleased with my digging; the way they carried on, one would have thought I was digging a hole to the center of the earth. I would even grow my own rock candy in the kitchen, studying its construction of crystallization. I would vow to save those beautiful clear crystals, but my taste buds would always get the best of me.

I fondly remember attending my first gem show: I was in the fifth grade. Pushing open the heavy metal doors, my eyes squinted from the bright lights as I stepped into a huge gymnasium. I heard a clamor and the sound of many voices—big people conversing, laughing, and asking questions. I was somewhat timid being with the grown-ups, but I was eager to see their world and discover their treasures that I hoped would become mine. Anxiously, I began to explore, looking to my left, then to my right, and back again. The energy tingling in my legs caused me to walk so fast that my eyes could not catch up. Flashing past, I saw hundreds of shiny stones: big ones, little ones, so many colors and shapes all uniquely displayed in glass jewelry cases.

People were gazing at the stones as if they were valuable treasures, and they carefully passed them to onlookers whose eyes seemed to open wide while their heads agreeably nodded with delight. Many put magnifiers to their eyes to get a closer look at the precious gems they adored. Money was passed over the top of the jewelry cases to the people who seemed to stand guard over the treasured stones.

The exciting discovery of free enterprise, as people became mesmerized by the beauty of the small, shiny objects—gems—was all so captivating to me, and I too found myself taken in by the entire gemstone splendor. My naive approach and wide eyes triggered a man's attention from behind one of the jewelry cases. He smiled.

Smiling back at him, I asked, "Where do all these gems come from?"

"They come from faraway places all over the world. Would you like to see one up close?"

"Oh yes, please," I said with my arm raised high and my palm extended out.

As he passed the stone over, my eyes lit up, just like the other grownups. Suddenly, I saw the most beautiful, awe-inspiring thing I had ever seen in my life. As I tilted my head, the stone glistened with flickers of light. Unexpectedly, it spoke to my heart in an unusual way, as if it knew me, as if we belonged together. Intrigued, I studied it, noticing that inside the stone were many tiny, triangular shiny things that resembled colorful glitter that seemed to dance with my imagination. I did not understand their luminous dance, but I wanted that gemstone as much as I believed it wanted me.

I asked, "What is it?"

"It is called goldstone."

"Goldstone? Why?"

"Because it looks like it's made from gold. Can you see the golden specks inside?"

I nodded my head yes.

"Those golden flakes create an illusion." With a poetic tone, he added, "The gem is cold to the touch but warm to the eye." Fascinated and puzzled, I asked, "Cold, warm, illusion?"

Realizing I was an inquisitive kid with a sincere interest, he tried to answer me with some science. "You see, the stone is really clear; it's those tiny metallic platelets inside the stone that cause you to see its pretty color."

Trying to make sense of what he said, I asked, "It's like magic?"

Smiling, he said, "Yeah, like magic."

Timidly, I asked, "How much for the stone?"

"Is this your first gemstone purchase?"

"Yes," I answered with enthusiasm.

Entertained by my childlike zeal, he playfully teased. Raising his eyebrows, he asked, "Did you know that once you buy your first gemstone, you open a door that will never close?"

"What do you mean?" I asked.

"Well, it's the door to new adventures."

Realizing that he had revealed a truth about himself with regard to his own profession, he hesitated briefly, and with genuineness he added, "The world of gems will take you on many journeys."

Pausing, his face became quite serious. "Are you ready to make that journey?"

"Oh yes!"

"So, what's it worth to you?

"I only have a dollar sixty-five!"

"Then the stone no longer belongs to me but to you. Bon voyage, little one."

That was my first gemstone purchase at the age of ten. I had sacrificed my life savings to buy the goldstone, but I walked away believing in my heart that everything in my life changed from that moment on. Every day I studied my stone, seeking answers, wondering how, what, why, and when would I leave on the journey the man spoke about. But for now, I would make it my lucky stone, taking it with me everywhere I went.

Little did I realize my gem purchase was a prelude to an onset of incredible journeys—not just to physical places, but into countless, true-life stories of many people.

Was it a coincidence that my first gemstone, goldstone, is also referred to as aventurine glass based on the original Italian name avventurina, from avventura, meaning *adventure* or *chance*?

CHAPTER 4
Discovering Destiny
Commitment and Discipline

Anne's father, Paul Ferrara, professional jazz drummer

I began to transition from childhood to young adulthood with the influence and support of the people around me, especially my large family. The need to share and do chores taught each of us about being considerate of others; never would anyone take the last of the milk without asking permission first.

With five young girls in the house, my sisters and I shared jeans and space, but we never shared boyfriends. While we did our chores in our small, 10' x 6' kitchen, we would turn up the radio, sing into a wooden spoon, and dance the latest jig. We shared one bathroom on a Friday night getting ready for "Mr. Right." As girls, we argued and often expressed our thoughts freely with one another. But within our core, we knew that no matter what, we would take care of each other. No one interfered with our sister-power, and to this day we are all very close.

My father was a strict Italian man who believed strongly in family and ingrained in us mottos like, "You do for your family" and "Family is always first." Even though my father was 5' 0" on a tall day, we feared him like a giant, especially when he revealed his "crazy eyes." "Crazy eyes" was his nonverbal expression when things weren't headed in his preferred direction. My dad was big on respect—always "yes sir," "no sir." When his crazy eyes and need for respect intersected, no one knew what he was capable of, or what was going to happen. For example, one time while watching television in his faded green leather reclining chair, he heard a car pull up in front of the house. Curious, he looked out the window of his domain and saw that the car had blocked his trash cans, the trash cans he strategically placed to be ready and waiting for city pick up. He got that look in his eyes and headed for the front door. With great force, he swung the door open and charged toward the car. Angrily, he lifted the cans and set them down onto the hood of that vehicle. My father feared no one.

My dad supported a family on a musician's salary—rich one week, poor the next. But my dad worked his true love, music, sometimes living from gig to gig. He was a well-known jazz musician who played for noted New Orleans icons, including Al Hirt, Pete Fountain, Louie Prima, Dukes of Dixieland, and so many others. To see my father perform on national television became a familiar excitement. He performed for many famous people, including four U.S. presidents, and even movie stars who would come to hear his New Orleans jazz drumming tempo. He was considered to be one of the best drummers in the world, and that is no exaggeration. His unique style of drumming is legendary in New Orleans jazz culture, never again to be captured in the same way.

Even though his talent was considered to be natural, he never took it for granted, practicing every day of his life, except Sundays.

If something disrupted his day or his schedule, I watched to see how he managed to still practice his drumming. His dedication and discipline meant that he would accept nothing less, and he would manage to squeeze in his daily rehearsal. My dad taught me many valuable lessons in life, but one great lesson was in regard to genuine happiness: do what you truly love for a living.

My father's bride, my mother, is a beautiful, full-blooded Irish lady from Brooklyn, New York, who has soft, creamy skin and a carefree attitude. My mother was all about her five girls and was determined that we experience the laughter and joy life had to offer, in ways both small and large. She kept an organized house, alternating spring curtains with fall curtains.

Because my mother married an Italian, she adopted the culture and lifestyle as if they were her own. Sunday dinners were truly Sunday Dinners. The Sunday dinner table was set more formally than during the week, and the best meals were served, like savory red gravy and perfectly-textured spaghetti and meatballs with a hint of garlic, topped with freshly grated cheese. On the side were vegetables mixed with melted cheeses and Italian bread crumbs, stuffed artichokes, crisp salad with cherry tomatoes, warm garlic bread, and a moist homemade yellow cake with chocolate icing. The entire neighborhood could smell our Sunday dinners from down the street. Mama's wisdom knew that the tradition of gathering together over a meal offered expressions of family love and unity. She expressed her own love through her generous care in preparation and serving, her steadfast emphasis on family, and her understanding that each person mattered to the group as a whole.

Mama was always home for the family. It was only later, when we were older and in high school, that she worked at an upscale ladies' clothing store. She always accessorized and dressed beautifully. She knew her customers by name and how to cater to them. Her attributes as an excellent employee surfaced quickly, and soon mom went from top sales clerk to manager of the store. She too was a role model for being a hard worker and detail-oriented while also looking great. Her hair was always neat, her makeup was not too heavy but natural-looking, and her gentle smile was an offer of warmth to anyone who glanced at her. My mother emanates a persona of always being pleasantly inviting, even to a stranger.

I learned from my parents the importance of character, work ethic, and the ability to recognize what is important in life. We united as one when hard times were upon the family of seven. Many a night, we would all gather on our knees and pray. If someone was ill, everyone was concerned and helped to do his or her chores. Siblings were not only sisters but our responsibility. My parents instilled in all of us the importance of always looking forward to the joys that life had to offer and to remember that the journey was just as important.

I got my first job when I was only thirteen. I scooped ice cream for $1.10 an hour. I can remember the manager being business-minded, periodically testing the weight of all the employees' scoops in order to make sure no one was giving away the profit. Because I loved being creative, I enjoyed the customers who would ask me to surprise them with something special. I would create a mountain of ice cream, piled high with glorious toppings, whipped cream, nuts, and a cherry. I was half Italian; how else was I expected to serve someone?

Moving up the food chain, my next job was at a grocery store. It was there that I was introduced to more lessons of life, such as the creative places where thieves could hide stolen food, namely inside their pants. I was often amazed, and sometimes taken aback, as I watched shoppers pull out their money from the most interesting nooks and crannies, such as quarters from the inside of their ears. It was intriguing to see how cleverly people tried to manipulate the government-subsidized food stamp system by trying to sneak nonfood items tucked under produce, hoping it would just slip on by without the notice of the cashier or grocery bagger. To collect change from such a system, many would repeatedly pass through the checkout line over and over again to gather as many quarters as possible. They were creating their opportunity at the tax payers' expense.

Wanting to polish my people skills, I took a photography job in a shopping mall, taking pictures of kids with Santa and the Easter Bunny. Holiday cheer was lacking many times when the Santa Claus did not show up or was inebriated. Immediately, I was on the phone calling in favors in exchange for a quick, sober Santa while in the background a line of screaming kids and unhappy parents waited impatiently. This job taught me how silly young parents can be, especially when they insisted that their three-day-old baby was capable of smiling for the camera. But more importantly, I learned that people wanted this experience with Santa. When their eyes filled with hope and excitement, it was suddenly worth the time and money they had invested.

I never really knew how to be still. I've worked since the day I was allowed. Even in middle and high school, I stayed very active with extracurricular activities, involving myself in just about everything except sports. I was coordinated but lacked self-confidence in my athleticism thanks to all the boys I grew up with in my neighborhood. I was in the math, speech, newspaper, and Beta clubs. I was on the student council and in cheerleading. I thrived on school competitions, from the talent shows to school projects, always seeking adventure with no fear.

Eventually, I felt I had more rewarding challenges to explore than school clubs—the working world. The idea of "real-world" compensation and self-worth had greater value to me than this kids' stuff. Fortunately, my high school offered Distributive Education which allowed high school students with enough academic credits to attend school for half the day and work the other half. It was a program made for a person like me. Not only did I participate in it, I became the president of the Distributive Education Club. This program focused on retail sales and marketing. I learned business terms and studied why and how people buy products. One important rule of the DE program: once you had a job, you had to keep it for the school year. This meant you could not get fired or quit, no exceptions. If you did, you were thrown out of the program and received a failing grade. The teacher in charge of the program explained this rule at least once a month, making it sound as if it would be better to have your fingernails pulled out than to be removed from the program. In her closing remarks, she always exclaimed, "It will be on your permanent record!" I could see her mouth move in slow motion, as if the mere sound of the words could give you a contagious disease. So I stuck it out with my jobs during the DE program. But truth be told, it taught me about job commitment and discipline. With that, I began to mature, and I was hoping my pocketbook would as well.

My job experiences and employment responsibilities went from sales clerk for a department store to clerical worker, then to a trusted bank teller, and by the legal age of eighteen, I earned my real estate license. Coincidentally, the first house I sold was equipped for someone with disabilities, including wheelchair accommodations from the kitchen counter tops and cabinets to the bidet toilet.

By twenty years old, I worked for a tax preparation company, completing personal and corporate taxes for people. It was strange because I often helped people who were older and more experienced in business. This put me in many awkward positions in an already high-pressure job, especially when clients declared me a savior or their worst enemy. No matter what I said, some thought me to be the Internal Revenue Service. Stares of disgust pierced me from across my desk while I informed them of the IRS rulings: "I'm sorry Mrs. Smith, but you cannot claim your pet as a dependent," and "No, Mr. Smith, your Trident gum is not deductible because you suffer from halitosis."

Despite the stress, this job presented an adventure every day. It was as if I had the privilege of interviewing hundreds of people, asking questions relevant to their tax preparation: number of dependents, status in life, employment, expenses, and assets. At times they shared more, such as their life's dreams. Some shared more than I bargained for, including detailed descriptions of their exes and their lovers. Money has a tendency to bring out people's emotions. It also gave me insight into the various talents people have, what they did or did not do with them, their compensation, the lack of monetary savings, and those who saved it for that rainy day as they shriveled up waiting for it to pour. I watched how people lied, and I noticed those who didn't. Self-employed people impressed me the most. I learned that some of the smartest people were in business for themselves, and without any Ivy League degree, they had a better understanding of business than most other people.

Steadfast, I remained committed and disciplined in my jobs because I believed with each job I was progressing toward a career opportunity, a journey yet to be unveiled. At times, the child in me gazed into my lucky goldstone, hoping and wishing something more in life would be discovered soon. I craved a profession that would make me whole.

Often, I questioned if I was waiting for life to come to me or if I was pressing forward to meet it.

CHAPTER 5
Entrepreneurial Seizures
God's Course Setters

A unique triple exposed picture from three separate events. From left to right, Anne's parents Paul and Diane Ferrara, Anne and Mike, Mike's parents Lois and Maestri Dale, and groomsman Leonard Davis on Anne and Mike's wedding day.

While waiting for my purpose in life to be revealed in God's time, I met someone special. In 1978, I began dating Michael Dale, now my husband of thirty years. Dating Mike was like hanging out with myself; we are similar in so many ways. During our dating days, we spent endless hours dreaming of future "entrepreneurial seizures" as to what we wanted to accomplish in our lives. We never tired of each other's company, and even when we weren't together, we were on the phone until all hours of the night. It was a time when telephones were still attached to the wall, usually in only one location of the house. For both of us, it was the kitchen. That meant the whole family could hear my every word during a phone conversation. With the receiver pressed to my ear, I would slide out of the chair onto the floor in uncontrollable laughter. Mike always made me laugh. While lying on that small kitchen floor, holding my stomach, cracking up hysterically, my four sisters would step over me, shaking their heads and laughing. They were probably guessing that I was in love. They were right.

At the end of every date, he walked me to mama's front porch. Since Michael was much taller than me, I would stand on the top porch step and he would stand on one lower. It would be there that we would romantically kiss, ending with an embrace, not wanting to let go. If we were out there too long, mama would turn on the bright, glaring porch light, putting a blinding, abrupt end to the night.

Are marriages made in heaven? I will never forget one special starry night. While we were arm-in-arm, there was a fast, brilliant shooting star racing across the night sky. I quickly sent my wish on the tail of that star, straight to the heavens. "I wish I'd marry Michael Dale," said the voice in my head. There on the porch, where the blind broom man stood so many years ago, I thought about a new magical ring that would bring Mike and me together forever. Three months later, I was engaged. At the innocent age of twenty, I married my best friend, Michael, and so we grew together, journeying toward the same goals—these ambitious, entrepreneurial concepts of ours.

Little did we know that God's "course setters" of opportunity were already knocking at our door, pointing us in the direction we would ultimately take in our careers. Of all things, it would be Mike who would take me beyond my childhood gem show experience and introduce me to the jewelry trade. Mike was persuaded by a family member to take a jewelry-making class as a pastime. Quickly, he discovered he had a natural talent in jewelry-making. Working tirelessly while apprenticing, he became a professional bench jeweler for several retail jewelry stores within a year. His shop was flourishing, and he asked for my partnership in business. Mike trained me, and together we quickly went from repairing jewelry at the bench to wholesaling regional custom designs. The jewelry business was our home, and we were a team. The artist in me desired to create fashion jewelry, which Mike supported. Encouraged by watching the blind broom man for many years, it was natural for me to adopt the salesperson role. I went door to door to retail stores, showing what we created with our hands.

During our struggles and successes, we contracted the "Self-Employment Disease." The symptoms are big dreams, hard work, perseverance, difficult decisions, risk-taking, and endless hope. Happy but miserable, I couldn't imagine living life any other way. The initial stages of building our business brought many financial challenges to our marriage. Some weeks offered as little as $15 to buy groceries, but it paid off in building character.

Additionally, being self-employed has other perks: you are your own boss, and you call all the shots. When it's good, it's a flowing fountain of endorphins, and with some saved spare change, you can buy something new for the house or just have a night out to dinner. But Self Employment Disease begs that any extra time or money be spent on another dream, another goal—it's always reinvested back into the business.

As young business risk-takers, our excitement overpowered our fear of failure; what a glorious way to live! Our struggles were great, but we believed our potential was even greater. Our endless quest of happy dreams for our future would never leave us.

Knowing that skill and knowledge are essential to any successful business, we enthusiastically searched for ways to learn more and reinvest in the business. While Mike continued to master his craft, I attended various types of jewelry conferences. It was at such a conference that I experienced an epiphany that would rock my world forever.

"Did you know that amethyst means 'not to intoxicate'?" said an interesting speaker who was also a gemologist. "This is why Bacchus, the Greek god, drank from an amethyst goblet while attending to business. By doing so, he could serve and drink as much wine as he wanted and not become drunk, while taking advantage of the others who did."

I had never met a gemologist, nor had I ever heard one speak. The gemologist discussed the fascinating lore and science of gemstones. Mesmerized, I became engrossed with the whole subject matter. I was where I was supposed to be in that moment of time. I knew then that I had the answer to the question I had asked my goldstone so many years ago: I was meant to be a gemologist. Appreciating the rarity of such a profound revelation, I quickly grabbed a pen and wrote, "I WILL BE A GEMOLOGIST."

A new journey had begun for me, and I explored an education as a gemologist. A gemologist is not a common expertise or career path. Many people confuse it with geology. A gemologist specializes in the scientific study of gems, and the profession has many facets. On a professional level, a gemologist scientifically identifies gems or is employed by jewelers, companies, or manufacturers as a buyer or seller of gems. Some become independent jewelry appraisers, researchers, writers, or teachers. Truth be told, on a personal level, a gemologist really is a rock hound with a gem of an appetite.

Many fascinating discoveries related to gems and their inherent beauty intrigued me. Amazed, I learned that gems are not only found in desolate deserts and volcanic terrain, but also as crystallizations in meteorites. Peridots and diamonds, for example, can be found hurtling through space. It fills one with a sense of awe. Some gems are millions of years old, taking a person back in time. A piece of amber might display a prehistoric insect in mid-action. Like magic, a scientific phenomenon in certain gems displays what looks like a cat's eye or a star as light penetrates and reflects off of the stone. But as captivating as some gems are, what's more amazing is the way they connect people around the world. They are treasures passed from one human hand to another, journeying through human hearts, intertwined with passion, power, and destiny.

I would soon embark on my journey of many discoveries as a gemologist. With only a few options in gemological education, I began my initial studies through a correspondence course, but my drive was moving faster than the snail-mail homework assignments. I needed to satisfy my gem of an appetite. I needed to be face to face with gems. I needed to sit in a classroom and immerse myself further in the subject. Unfortunately, there were very, very few gemology schools to choose from in the United States. Luckily for me, fate would intervene.

In Dallas, Texas in 1986, while passing time before a seminar, curiosity walked me over to a table that was stacked two feet high with copies of a gemology book. I saw no one around, but heard this dry, commanding voice from behind the stack.

"It's a good book. Buy it. You might learn something."

Leaning over the stacks, I saw this balding man staring at me through his black-rimmed glasses. He didn't smile. He didn't frown. He was a man of no nonsense, and his appearance resembled a university professor. Not responding to him, I cautiously picked up the book, flipped it over, and noticed that the man with the authoritative voice looked exactly like the author's photo on the back flap. He had no idea that I was a student of gemology, anxiously looking to further my studies on a more scientific level. A social man he was not, but in our brief conversation, he did mention his gemology school in Maryland. I asked about possible employment. It turned out that he just happened to need a typist in his jewelry appraising lab. I could practically hear the sound of opportunity knocking, and I immediately responded.

"I just happen to be a typist."

The truth was that I really wasn't a secretarial typist, but I had confidence that I could learn quickly.

It turned out that this man would not be just another person in the jewelry business; he was Antonio Bonanno, one of the most prestigious, well-known gemologists in the industry. Not only did he own a gemology school, but he also operated a gemological laboratory and jewelry appraising business. Miraculously, he would become my mentor.

Meanwhile, I had pressing issues to deal with, like telling Mike that I was moving to Maryland for a little while to study gemology. I called Mike from Texas and shared with him the opportunities I had discussed with Mr. Bonanno. Knowing me too well, he realized my determination and reluctantly agreed. With a grateful heart, I booked a one-way ticket to Silver Spring, Maryland.

CHAPTER 6
The Gemologist
Building Character

Anne presenting Mr. Bonanno with a lifetime achievement award
on behalf of the Gemmological Association of Great Britain.

Excited and inexperienced at living on my own, I forged ahead, stuffing two suitcases with one place setting, one pot to cook with, a blanket, one set of sheets, soap, a towel, some notebooks, and clothing. Mike brought me to the airport. We embraced with heavy, concerned hearts, but I knew it was something I had to do. My drive to succeed was bigger than me.

Beyond the challenges of studying the science of gemology, I would have to put forth effort in fostering characteristics that were needed in order to achieve my goal. First and foremost, I was going to need perseverance and discipline. Success would require that I overcome new obstacles and face humility at times, but collectively the experience would make for a sweeter triumph.

SWEPT AWAY

Being a southern girl, my arrival in Maryland began with a stressful and unfamiliar scene—a snow storm. As the plane prepared for landing, flight attendants announced the cancelation of connecting flights and ground transportation. I knew I was far away from the comfort of home when I looked out the plane's window and saw the snow-blanketed runway. The airport came to a standstill, and I had no time to waste. Miserably cold, I walked, gracelessly pulling my survival luggage through the slush outside in search of transportation. As snow accumulated on my eyelashes, I desperately hoped for the appearance of a cab. There was not one in sight, just as the flight attendants had warned. It was a Friday evening, nearing five o'clock, and I was feeling Maryland's wet, cold initiation. Pressure was mounting—I had to get to the office of my newly-leased, unseen apartment before it closed. With bad weather and very little money, there was no allowance for an alternative place over the weekend, nor did I want to spend my first few days sleeping in an airport.

Luck surfaced, and I spotted the parking lights of a cab in the distance. Because of the storm's intensity, I sensed I would have to put my bargaining skills to work. Heading towards the cab driver, I put on my pitiful facial expression that said, "Please, please may I have your sympathy? I'm helpless." With a southern charm, I proceeded to ask if he would be so kind as to help me. I hardly began my plea when he abruptly replied, "Not in this weather."

I decided it would be better to cut to the chase with a straightforward approach. Deepening my voice, I asked, "How about double the fare?"

At first he laughed in disbelief, but when he realized my young-looking face meant business, he joyously smirked and agreed. With little visibility, he drove very slowly. He was busy conversing on the cab radio, sometimes in English, sometimes not. I was surprised when suddenly his driving pace picked up and for some reason he embraced a new sunshiny attitude. He pulled over and picked up what seem to be a close acquaintance—his buddy—on my nickel.

"It will just take a minute, it is on the way," he said.

I pleaded, "I don't have time for this," my concern being ignored.

His friend sat in the front seat. They carried on a busy conversation in a language foreign to me. They exchanged a laughter that indicated life was just a peach. I could only imagine that they were laughing at me, the desperate southerner who was paying double the fare.

This future gemologist was between a rock and hard place, grateful for the snow ride but aggravated that my urgent situation was not respected—or my nickel. It was stress on top of stress. The only relief I got was to loudly sigh every time they broke out into a burst of laughter. Somehow, I made it to the apartment's management office with only three minutes to spare. Ready to collect double fare, the cab driver quickly threw my bags onto the sidewalk. But now it was my turn.

"I will be right back to pay you."

His satisfied expression transformed into worry.

As I hurried toward the office, I flippantly shouted, "Uh huh, let's see who's laughing now."

Trying not to slip in the snow with my tennis shoes, I raced towards the office door and there stood the manager, blocking the doorway with his arms folded. I surmised by his unwelcoming body language that he wanted to leave work early due to the snow. "Here's your key, Ms. Louisiana. Sign here."

With a wave of his hand in a general direction, he said, "Your apartment is up the road."

Agitated by the journey's events, along with his rudeness, I sarcastically smiled and asked him with an exaggerated southern drawl, "And what state would I be in?" implying that this wasn't the warm south.

Insensitive and unaffected by my implication, he handed me a map of the apartment complex. I paid the waiting cab driver the double fare but no tip. I bid him and his friend farewell—"Hasta la vista, baby"— and off they drove.

To this rural girl, the apartment complex was huge, and each separate apartment building looked exactly the same . . . dreary, plain, and lonely.

With my apartment a few blocks uphill, I dragged my suitcases once again through the wet snow. By then, I had begun to discover a new temperature, a cold chill that reached beyond my bones and wet feet. With my key in hand, I unlocked the door that led to a gloomy, frigid, echoing, one-bedroom apartment.

I was second-guessing my decisions as the squeaky door closed behind me. Reality hit me like a pie in the face. The noise of silence screamed, and there I was alone with my two suitcases. Sitting on top of them, I sobbed tears of regret.

"What am I doing here? I don't know anyone. These people are not friendly. I'm a newlywed, and I left my husband for this. I'm so used to being around my large family—no more pasta on Sundays, no phone, no television. I don't even know where the grocery store is."

The clouds quickly darkened the night sky. Cellular phones didn't exist at that time, and I didn't have a landline installed yet. With no one to talk to and no furniture to sit on, I laid my winter coat on the parquet floor, curled up, and tried to sleep. After the long, cold night, the morning sun eventually rose and I ventured out to explore my new neighborhood. I found a grocery store and a pay phone. I placed a collect call to Mike.

"I made it," I proclaimed, trying not to sound daunted.

Monday arrived, and I anxiously made my way to Mr. Bonanno's gemological and appraisal lab. Curious and eager to talk with someone, I asked my new coworkers a variety of questions regarding gemology, the town, and furniture stores, but I remained quiet about my loneliness, embarrassed that I might seem needy. A coworker, realizing that I needed furniture, graciously lent me a cot and took me to a furniture-rental store.

I put in long days. My schedule consisted of working in Mr. Bonanno's lab during the day, attending both his beginners and advanced classes in the evenings, as well as studying for two additional gemological correspondence courses before bed each night. Exhausted at times, I would rest my head on the typewriter at my desk for a few minutes, only to be awakened by a startling, shockingly-loud banging sound. Quickly lifting my head, I would rub my eyes and see a huge gemology book that had been dropped on the desk beside my sleeping head. In the distance, I would see "the man," my boss, walking away from me.

My mentor, my boss of few words, generously gave me his support and offered his time to teach me the science of gemology. He became more than my teacher; he was like a grandfather. He was brilliant. I held him in high regard, even if he went out of his way to affectionately embarrass me in the presences of clients. Often he would call me into his office, hand me a piece of jewelry, and ask in his authoritative voice, "What gemstone is in this ring? Identify it."

Then he would add, "You'd better get it right, or you can go back to Louisiana."

Nervously, I would examine the stone, carefully looking for clues that would give me an answer. Most of the time, he only allowed me to use a jeweler's loupe to make my determination.

"You can't carry a microscope in your pocket everywhere you go. You can see plenty with your eyes. Use your brain and your jeweler's loupe. Look hard. Think, girl, think!" he would demand.

He wanted me to process my observations by relying on natural abilities, as if my eyes and brain were the gem equipment. With the jeweler's loupe, he was teaching me his techniques to identify certain gem properties visible to the eye of a skilled gemologist. I would give my best guess, and he would then ask, "Why?"

With him a lucky guess was not acceptable. He demanded a scientific answer as to how one reached his or her conclusion. He knew his field of gemology and much more; he was a chemist and geologist. Many people within the industry relied on his expertise—students, jewelers, industry leaders, publishers, and even the Smithsonian Institute.

My job didn't pay much, but it was there, under his guidance, that I had the privilege of being exposed to a unique opportunity in gemological education. With a salary barely covering my rent and utilities, I was left with a weekly grocery budget that afforded me cheap instant coffee, scrambled eggs, and pan-fried potatoes. Some nights my hungry stomach made it difficult to fall asleep. At dusk, I had one light bulb burning in the entire apartment. I dared not spend any money on another bulb when I could buy food instead!

Money worries and intensive study took their toll on me. I lost weight and began to develop a gray patch of hair, dead center in the front portion of my scalp. All I could credit it to was that my brain was responding to the overload of work and study.

Even though Mr. Bonanno's personality appeared insensitive at times, I knew he was concerned for my well-being. As he observed my weight loss, he tried to communicate this in his unique way by referring to me as "fat girl." He often asked if I needed an advance on my pay or would offer to share his most treasured dessert, ice cream.

To add to my stress, my Italian father would write to me at least once a week. His letters would plead, "Come home. You should be with your husband and family. We miss you." His correspondence included handwritten novena prayers—nine pages long. I knew where he was coming from—tradition—but I knew I had to do this for me. I had to pass my exams. I had worked hard, investing all my time and believing that my reputation, my pride, and my future were on the line. I had to prove to myself that I was meant to be a gemologist.

As with my father, Mr. Bonanno's toughness was just on the surface; in reality, he had a heart of gold. He wanted me to succeed. He knew I had traveled far and sacrificed much to accomplish my goal. More importantly, he saw something in me, more than I saw in myself—a good gemologist. He changed my life.

Back home, Mike was working long hours, and alone, he was sustaining the business. We wished we could see each other, but neither one of us had any spare change with which to buy a plane ticket. We would learn that the cliché "distance makes the heart grow fonder" is true. With my heart aching from missing Mike, I had to brainstorm an idea to get home to see him. Then one day it came to me as I walked past a restaurant in downtown Silver Spring. I saw a sign advertising a shrimp dinner that was expensively priced, at least to me, a Louisiana girl. People in the north paid dearly for fresh shrimp, but back home they were a dime a dozen. Risking a portion of my salary, I bought a round-trip ticket home. My idea required marketing and preselling a product—Gulf shrimp—that I didn't own, at least not yet. I managed to get a few committed buyers, and after my visit home, I returned to Maryland with fresh, reasonably priced Louisiana shrimp.

Mike and I greeted each other like that typical couple you see in an airport, hugging and kissing. Reuniting with Mike, the family, and mama's pasta made me long for home even more. But before I knew it, with tears in my eyes and shrimp in hand, I headed back to my lonely, one-light-bulb apartment. I had to focus, succeed in my gemological education, and deliver any presold shrimp to quickly make up the difference to pay my rent.

Before unpacking my suitcase, I immediately de-headed the shrimp, weighed them, and packaged them by the pound. Setting up before an evening gemology class of Mr. Bonanno's, I wrote on the chalkboard, "Anne's back in town . . . SHRIMP FOR SALE—REASONABLY PRICED, 'DE-HEADED' too." I managed a few trips back home to New Orleans with this endeavor. I was now in the seafood business—who would have ever dreamed?

As I studied and prepared, I anxiously waited for exam day to arrive. In order to complete some of my correspondence and classroom gemology courses, I took a series of exams under the guidance of Mr. Bonanno, all of which took place over the course of a three-day span. One particular and important exam was from the prestigious Gemological Association of Great Britain. They carried the reputation of having the highest distinction in gemological education in the world. They are referred to as a Harvard or Yale of gemological studies. They teach the "whys" of gemology, everything from beauty and rarity to the detailed science behind it. Their alumni included gemological authors, scientists, and gem gurus from around the world. Anyone who was someone in the field of gemology had his or her diploma from the association, and that was what I desired. Of course, Mr. Bonanno was among the very few who had earned such a diploma with a distinction classification under their banner.

In the 1980s, the British course and exam were not geared toward Americans. Proudly, it seemed to me, they had granted fewer than fifty diplomas in the United States, none of which were in my home state. In order to pass the Brits' exam, a student had to achieve a standardized grade of A or B; C did not constitute a passing mark.

Before the scheduled exam days, Maryland experienced two distracting and unusual phenomena. The first phenomenon was the Year of the Locust which naturally occurs every seventeen years. Freakishly large, black locusts with red eyes emerged from the ground and swarmed the area. I think they were waiting for my arrival before they invaded the town. Crunch, crunch under the soles of shoes was a familiar sound on the city sidewalks, as was the sight of people swatting madly in the air, tormented by these little black demons. They fluttered about, tangling hairdos, landing on cars, even flying into your mouth if you opened it wide enough to scream. Everywhere I looked, I saw scenes reminiscent of the movie *The Birds* by Alfred Hitchcock.

The other phenomenon was an unusual heat wave that even caused this southern girl to feel its discomforts. The heat arrived and remained during the three long days of my exams. With only one window and a broken air conditioner, the exam room became a sauna. To top it off, the examination consisted of a handwritten questionnaire that required a student to use British spelling, and it needed to be legibly handwritten. Mr. Bonanno thought that by turning out all the lights except for the flexible bench lamp above my head, I would keep cool. I was spot-lit under the intense light fixture. After several sweaty hours, I could feel creases form the number 11 in the skin of my brow as I wrinkled my forehead with stress and concentration. I felt as if I were on trial for everyone to view. Repeatedly, I rubbed my bent neck for relief. With every thought of failing, sweat rolled down my forehead and down the length of my back. As I tried to concentrate, out of the darkness of my imagination came my father, giving me the "Italian guilt look," my husband motioning for me to come home, and the rest of the family eating spaghetti and meatballs, staring as if I were their entertainment. I proofread my examination answers over and over, trying desperately to focus. I gave it all I had. I put the pen down and handed over the tests that represented the past year of sacrifices and endless study. It would be months before I would receive the results of my exam from England. In the meantime, it was time for me to move back home to Louisiana.

I packed up my things and said my farewells to everyone. Emotionally torn, I said my goodbyes to a man who helped re-shape my destiny. He was my mentor and my friend. I knew I would miss Mr. Bonanno. He brought forth a hidden self-confidence that existed under my young, girly persona. I had gained his respect. I walked away a professional gemologist, knowing that specialists respectfully remain students and educators throughout their entire careers, graciously sharing their knowledge with others. I had arrived in Maryland cold and timid in the midst of a blizzard, and thanks to him, I left with a heated confidence. I had weathered a storm.

Months passed, and finally the envelope arrived from England with my exam results. Quietly sitting alone in my living room, I placed the sealed envelope on the coffee table. Resting my goldstone that journeyed with me for years next to it, I found myself pensively starring at them both for about thirty minutes, playing out two scenarios. A passing mark would impact my career, and I would soar further than I could imagine. That was what my heart really wanted. A failing mark would crush my dreams, my confidence, and I would be lost as to the direction of my life, at least for a while, but I would still be me. However, I would have to start all over again.

I carefully opened the envelope, and the powerful word PASS leaped from the page. Standing straight up with gratification, I then dropped to my knees with humility and thanked God. I felt satisfied that I had achieved my goal, the most difficult goal thus far. I now held a diploma from the most prestigious gemological association in the world and was the first designated "Fellow of the Gemmological Association of Great Britain" in Louisiana. I cried, overwhelmed with joy. Clenching my goldstone, I picked up the phone to call my mentor. His dry but proud response was, "Of course you passed." He never doubted my ability.

I kept in touch with Mr. Bonanno and always made it a point to visit him at trade events. His door and heart were always open to me.

Years later, I received the phone call I never wanted. He had died. I attended his funeral and said farewell to someone who meant so much to me. He is now among the greatest jewels in heaven. His spirit stays with me today, and whenever I pick up a stone to identify, I hear his voice echoing, "What is that stone, and more importantly, why?"

He inspired me to journey endlessly, pursue education and research, and travel internationally. He introduced me to both the past and future worlds of gemology that led me to the "Diamond People" and more.

I learned many lessons with my move to Maryland, but most importantly, the experience taught me about character. It's not something you can buy or pass on; you have to earn it.

CHAPTER 7
Crossing the Neutral Ground
Entrusting Gifts

Anne with a diamond cutter in Antwerp

Saint Charles Avenue in New Orleans is "The Avenue." It is lined with great old oak trees and grand mansions. It is also divided by a "neutral ground"—a slang term used by New Orleanians to indicate a dividing line between their side and someone else's. In reality, it is a strip of land stationed in the middle of the street that separates a two-way road. On The Avenue's neutral ground, the famed historic New Orleans streetcars parade Uptown and Downtown. Ever since I was a little girl, I always wondered who lived behind those large, columned-porch homes. Soon after I became a professional gemologist, I met such a person.

With my gemology degrees in hand, I divided my time between working in the jewelry shop with Mike and evaluating jew-

48

elry independently for jewelry stores and private individuals. One day I received a phone call from a lady requesting an appointment to have her jewelry appraised. She said she didn't drive and asked if I would travel to her home. She happened to live on the beautiful Saint Charles Avenue. When the appointment time came, I have to admit, I was very excited. Standing on the porch in front of the ornate entryway, I searched for the doorbell that seemed to be hidden within the fancy wrought-iron work. It had to be somewhere. Wondering what the blind man would do in such a situation, I knocked, and just like him, I listened for an answer. I heard the sound of footsteps approach, and the door opened. There stood a white, pristine, tidy maid in uniform. I introduced myself, and she escorted me into a huge, dimly-lit living room. The twenty-foot ceiling, intricate crown molding, two marble fireplaces, and four-columned room painted quite a grand sight for a girl who grew up in a small three-bedroom house. In the back darkened corner of the room sat a stately, elderly woman wearing a blue dress and large chandelier, diamond earrings. Carefully, she stood up with the aid of a cane.

She introduced herself. "Hello! My name is Ms. Valerie Laurent."

"Hello, I'm Anne Dale."

"Please, sit down. Would you care for some tea?" she asked.

Seeing that the tea was already prepared, I wanted to be polite. "Yes, thank you."

"Would you be a dear and pour it please . . . Did you have to travel a long distance to get here?"

Looking around the room, thinking of the path I had traveled in my gemological studies that brought me to this side of the neutral ground, I wanted to respond, "Oh you bet." But I knew better.

"No, not really."

"How long have you been in the jewelry business?"

"I have been in the industry for a little over five years."

"I know it's impolite to ask someone their age, but you sound young."

"I don't mind. Twenty-four."

"Well, you came highly recommended by Mr. Shemberg, the auctioneer in New Orleans. I understand you have several distinctions in your field, including one from England. Sounds impressive. Please tell me about your credentials."

I had no qualms being interviewed, so I elaborated.

"I am designated as a Fellow of the Gemological Association of Great Britain, which is considered to be the highest diploma distinction in gemological education. I'm also a Professional Gemologist from the Columbia School of Gemology and a Graduate Gemologist from the Gemological Institute of America."

"Please tell me what does a gemologist do?"

"I participate in many diverse aspects in my field, including appraising, identifying, researching, writing, tutoring, brokering, buying, and selling. With regard to appraising, I appraise for individuals, jewelry stores, companies, and the Internal Revenue Service."

"You have an interesting accent too, a little Yankee-sounding. Tell me about your family and where your people are from."

Smiling, I said, "You are correct. My mother is from Brooklyn, New York, and my father is from New Orleans. Mom was an airline stewardess when she met daddy, a jazz musician."

Her inquiries were made in an effort to find common ground, a need to feel comfortable, and establish a form of trust; jewelry is a very personal thing. I had no reservations revealing that I was just me, someone not from money. I was from a strong family structure, and my parents taught me to hold my head up. In fact, I took pride in being raised with less. It demonstrated that I appreciated nice things.

"I grew up in a small home in Kenner with four sisters. We shared most things, including the responsibly of caring for each other, especially when my parents worked. My mother manages the Gus Myer clothing store. I'm sure you're familiar with it. My father is a jazz drummer who performs at a variety of venues such as the Maison Bourbon and the Famous Door—mostly places in the French Quarter. My parents ingrained in us five girls that education was a privilege, not a right. I married young, to someone like-minded, Michael. My husband is also in the jewelry business as a master jeweler, and we work together.

"Ms. Laurent, please rest assured that if your jewelry is beyond my expertise, I promise I will let you know immediately. My reputation is important to me."

There was a quiet moment. Sipping my tea and wanting to end the silence, I stated, "You have a beautiful house."

"Thank you . . . my, five sisters?"

The tone of her voice was that of approval.

"How blessed you are to be part of a large family!"

Her shielded greeting had peeled away, and trust stepped forward.

She let out a sigh as if she had to confess something, something that would bring about a different reason as to why I was there.

"I've been married three times. I have two children who live out of state. Unfortunately, they only visit me about once a year."

Reaching for my hand, she confided, "What I am about to tell you, most people Uptown don't know." Hesitating, she continued, "I am sure you noticed there are no lights on, and that my makeup consists of just lipstick . . . Sadly, I have lost my sight. I am blind."

I was surprised by her confession; I didn't notice. But now it all made sense to me. That explained why she was in tune to my young voice that had an accent and her request that I pour the tea. I searched for any words that might comfort this lady of strong character. The only immediate sentiment I managed to express was, "I am sorry."

"Thank you," she replied.

She called out to her maid to bring her jewelry box.

"You see my late husband died about five years ago. He always adorned me with exquisite jewelry."

As she exhaled, there was a sound of disappointment.

"But now . . . I must sell it. I have become what some consider a recluse. Financially, I need to keep my estate afloat. I am hoping that you can help me."

Her maid placed the jewelry box on the small table between us. Opening it carefully, Ms. Laurent pulled out a ten-carat diamond solitaire ring, about the size of a quarter. Gently feeling the details of the ring with her fingertips, she stated, "I can only touch the jewelry and recall its beauty in my memories."

Eager to share more with me, she searched the box and found a ruby and diamond bracelet. Running it through the palm of her hand, she said, "I remember the night he gave this to me . . . I had on a gold-colored dress."

As she handed me the bracelet, she began to reminisce. "It was one of those crisp nights nearing the holidays where you feel there is something magical in the air. We were going to Galatoire's for dinner; that was our favorite restaurant, and I love their shrimp remoulade and the bread pudding . . . Oh my, listen to me go on."

"The bracelet is stunning. The workmanship is impressive, truly a one of a kind. He must have had it custom made for you," I replied.

Again feeling around in the box, she reached for another from her collection. "Now this one is my favorite. It is the smallest diamond ring I own, but it is very dear to my heart. It is from my first husband." With a whisper and a smile she added, "He really was my first love."

As she sat quietly reflecting on a memory, she rubbed it delicately. Tears welled up in her eyes.

"We were only married for two years when he died tragically in an automobile accident."

Handing me the ring, she said, "I'm sure you won't be impressed with its size, but for me, there was always something special about it."

"Ms. Laurent, it is not the size of the gift, but the size of the heart that gives it . . . This diamond is very beautiful. It has incredible fire, reflecting a great deal of brilliance . . . May I tell you a story?"

"Please."

I continued. "Often, I wonder about the first man who discovered the original diamond and how he revealed its beauty in its true form. In my imagination, I concluded that it must have happened something like this . . .

It's early morning. Imagine the panoramic view down in a valley that is protected by mountainous terrain: the dawning sun, the rolling green pastures, and the dew that beads up delicately on the vegetation. It's a sanctuary of peace. There in the valley lives a man who stands tall, works his farm, and tends to his sheep. Part of his daily routine is to guide his sheep to the green, hilly pastures for grazing. For him, this task is one of the more relaxing duties of his day. Because he converses with his sheep, some of the locals in the nearby town criticize him for his gentle demeanor. They are mistaken—he is quietly wise. He knows the land well and appreciates all that it has to offer. He also understands that nature demands respect.

As the sun begins to shine, he looks up at it to keep track of the day. He knows his thirsty sheep need a drink of water. Steering them to the river, he takes a break too. To cool his feet he wades into the shallow part of the river. Looking down into the water, he sees a brilliant object that is twinkling next to his worn leather sandal, as if it is calling to him. The strange glistening object is unlike anything the land as ever shown him before. Intrigued, he studies it further and bends down to reach for it, but suddenly he feels a strange, tingling sensation travel up his arm. He pauses but is not deterred by the feeling and proceeds to pick up the foreign-looking object.

Curiously, he studies it; his intuition tells him it's mysteriously special, but he doesn't know why. He is unaware that the brilliant object he holds is man's discovery of the first diamond ever. It is at this time in history that the diamond has chosen to reveal its existence, and he will be the first of the diamond people.

However, the diamond will need to reveal its power before one can appreciate its purpose for the world. As he rotates the shiny object, it sparkles with a refreshing beauty, reflecting a magnificent spectrum of bright blues, reds, yellows and oranges. The more he stares into it, the more it reveals. Suddenly, the very center of the diamond ignites, glowing as if it were alive. Captivated and seeking an understanding, he raises the diamond closer to the level of his eyes. Its radiance intensifies. Looking into it, he sees a vision of nature's power: a volcano erupting, spewing out fiery flames and lava and unmercifully burning everything that surrounds it. The air around him is sweltering, burning his oxygen. Sweat beads form on his forehead. The temperature of the diamond changes; it scorches his hand. Dropping it to the ground, he gasps to breathe and steps away from it.

As it hits the ground, the vision leaves him and the diamond cools, transforming back to its desirable beauty. Helplessly, he finds himself still tugged by a strange attraction to the diamond. Watchful, he steps toward it again, knowing that it possesses an incredible strength and it has survived nature's fury, being the hardest natural substance he has encountered.

Cautiously and barely touching the diamond, he gently places the tip of his finger on it. But in that one delicate connection, something significant is revealed: it's the wisdom that such a rare treasure can evoke deadly greed in a man, but only if he allows it to enter his heart. It is a greed that can root itself in the darkest part of the human spirit . . . sometimes never finding its way out.

Confident he is not among such men, he chooses to pick it up and thus he begins to experience the effects of such greed as it starts to consume him mentally and physically. His features transform, and the whites of his eyes blacken. With wicked lust, he clutches the diamond. He looks around, making sure that no one else wants to take what he has. Wanting to keep it to himself, he runs behind a tree where he can adorn himself with the beautiful object in secret. Possessed with his treasure, his mind's eye sees a horrifying vision—men fighting, stealing, and murdering one another because of self-inflicted greed.

A goodness that still exists in a portion of his heart overpowers his evil, and he is stunned by the reality that he himself was among such men. By the grace of God, his wise and gentle nature is redeemed. Letting go of the object once again, he drops the diamond to the ground. Cradling his head and crying with remorse, he believes the brilliant object is cursed. Wanting no part of it, he slowly backs away. Stumbling, he trips and hits his head on a rock. Everything becomes silent; his eyes close and time disappears.

When he awakens, he is somewhat dazed. Sitting up, he looks around, wondering what happened. He hears the peaceful, familiar sounds of nature. His sheep are drinking from the river. Looking up at the sun, he sees that it seems to be in the same position. He rubs his sore head feeling for a bump. Perplexed, he wonders if he has been dreaming the whole time, but it all seemed so real. Feeling emotionally and physically fatigued, he carefully rises to his feet to head home but spots a light gleaming from the shallow end of the riverbed . . . just as before.

Wanting answers to the mystery, he walks toward it. Moved by its familiar beauty, he wades into the water and slowly falls to his knees. Carefully scooping it into his cupped calloused hands, he stares at the diamond's wondrous splendor. His rapid beating heart invites in its mystery, and a revelation unfolds. In the diamond's final conquering state, it shares with him its purpose—it has come to celebrate love, bringing together millions of people, generation after generation, young and old. He has been entrusted with a significant gift, the first diamond, and with such a gift, man must be aware of its strength, power, and beauty.

Holding the treasured gift close to his chest, he runs home to his love. He throws the door open with excitement and stands speechless. His facial expression alone announces that he has something exceptional that he wants to present to her. Anticipating her response, he slowly opens his hands, his eyes focused upon her. He presents her a treasured gift from his heart: the first diamond ever.

"So you see, Ms. Laurent, my fictional story of the first diamond discovered illustrates many truths. It is in how we approach things in life that we receive gifts, and it is in how we present them that they are received. But more importantly, it is to whom we give them to that their true value is revealed."

CHAPTER 8

De Beers and the Diamond People

Shared Passion

Anne with world-renowned diamond cutter, Gabi Tolkowsky

U p until 1993, the only thing besides my British Gemology Distinction I had in common with England was the tea bags in my kitchen pantry. I never dreamed I would encounter the renowned Diamond People—De Beers.

Because it was natural for me to share my passion about gemstones, I began teaching educational seminars to a variety of audiences, from school kids to professionals in the jewelry trade. Inspired by the attendees' interest, I found myself encouraging those who expressed a desire to pursue an education in gemology. I knew that the Gemological Association of Great Britain offered the best education, but I was also aware of the fact that Americans had limited access to their method of teaching. I suddenly had an "entrepreneurial seizure." I approached and sold the Brits on the concept that they needed an American representative—me. They agreed, and I set out to expand gemological education through existing colleges and trade schools in the U.S. To do so, I contracted American tutors to help with the numerous correspondence courses.

My new position brought about unique gemological opportunities, giving me insight into both the business and politics of the diamond industry. The Association has always had a long-standing relationship with De Beers. When you think De Beers, you think diamonds, and diamonds are a driving force in the worldwide jewelry industry. De Beers' rich history would make my first visit to the company's headquarters in London a dream come true.

In October of 1992, the CEO of the Gemological Association of Great Britain had arranged for me a special visit to De Beers' Central Selling Organization (CSO). It's one of the few places in the world where gem quality rough diamonds are sorted into categories to be classified, valued, and then sold to diamond cutters worldwide. Ultimately, these cut diamonds are set in jewelry, thus making their way to consumers. The organization maintains a strategic balance between supply and demand, ensuring stability for the world's diamond supply.

When the CEO and I arrived at the CSO, they placed us in a waiting room. Most of the walls in the room were mirrored. The CEO informed me that we had to wait for about twenty minutes—my anticipation made it feel as though I would have to wait for hours. He told me "they" were listening to our conversation and monitoring our behavior through hidden cameras that were behind the mirrors. This was part of the vetting process before we could officially go in. It might have been routine for him, but it was major excitement for me.

In the room was a framed photo of a De Beers' mine in South Africa. As I stared into the old picture, my thoughts were swept into the past, reflecting on the people, the diamond people, and those who revolutionized the diamond industry. De Beers' influential and powerful insights began in the late 1800s when South Africa became the most important diamond mining location in the world. During that "diamond rush" period, anyone could purchase their own prospecting land and establish their own diamond mining company. Individuals could also purchase available shares with some of the existing mining companies. Such possibilities attracted many private diggers, but prospectors would eventually need to invest in more sophisticated and expensive mining operations that required specialized equipment, knowledge, and workers. This expensive overhead caused many of them to falter financially and sell outright, eliminating private diggers altogether. This essentially left two influential and savvy business men who owned and operated the South African diamond mines, Barney Barnato and Cecil Rhodes. Rhodes and Barnato battled to own all the diamond mines in South Africa, trying to buy out investors and each other. Their personal war was not only known throughout the local town, but all over the world by international investors. Ultimately, these mines would become known as the most significant and famous diamond mines in history. Their determination, decisions, and story affected the way the world perceives the value of diamonds today—from every jeweler to every person who wears a diamond. Even I feel connected to them.

Ambitious Barney Barnato was a hard worker and well-known character. He grew up in London, working numerous jobs, from circus acrobat to first-rate boxer. Wanting to be a diamond-mine owner, he arrived in South Africa at the age of eighteen with sixty boxes of cigars as his negotiating capital. He was described by some as uneducated, arrogant, and unscrupulous, but to others, he was a gentleman. Regardless, he possessed the extraordinary gift to make money. His perseverance paid off, and he fulfilled his dream to become a powerful and very rich businessman, forming the Barnato Mining Company.

Conservative Cecil Rhodes had financial backing. He was highly-educated and polished. In 1880 Rhodes formed the De Beers Mining Company, Ltd. after purchasing farmland from the De Beer family. The land, rich in diamond deposits, became synonymous with the famed name De Beers.

With his patient, polished character and huge financial support, Rhodes eventually won the diamond war and bought Barnato out. In 1888, Rhodes gained further control, merging several mines to form the De Beers Consolidated Mines, Ltd. He now had major control over marketing policies and exporting, both of which helped to create the diamond industry we know today.

Barnato, revered as one of the wealthiest men in the world, continued to develop prosperous business opportunities. His interest still remained in Africa, where he owned and operated the Rand Gold Fields. His power and success were envied by many. It was said that those who didn't like him went out of their way to work against him. Sadly, in 1897, the Jewish Chronicle reported that a telegram from Funchal, Maderia stated that Barnato, at the age of forty-four, had thrown himself overboard from the Union Liner's Scott as it was heading home to England. Although there were speculations of suicide, his death remains very mysterious. His body was recovered and buried in England.

I stared into that old photograph, lost deep in my thoughts, forgetting for a second where I was. Then I heard a door open, and my eyes shifted away from the photo and onto the reflective glass where I could see that my escort had arrived. In the blink of an eye, I traveled through hundreds of years of history, from that old mine to this incredible modern facility. Venturing on our way, we passed through certain entryways where security greeted us by announcing our names loudly for recording purposes. It reminded me of something from a James Bond movie.

The CEO, who frequently visited the company, left me to tour with a De Beers' public relations marketing officer who was a contact person between the CSO and gemological laboratories around the world. He struck me as well-educated and very English. His mannerisms were those of someone who was weary from his life's routine and who enjoyed escaping with a Scotch whiskey. He wore glasses and a three-piece suit, his dyed hair was slicked back, his lips were cracked and dry, and his teeth were those of a heavy smoker. His deep, gravelly voice seemed to reveal a stressful and secret life. I sensed my visit was a break, a relief from his high pressure job. One of the rooms he brought me into had piles of diamonds on several tables. Because of the tight security and cameras, I was terrified to move my hands much less my body. Such a sight made it difficult for me to contain myself. The voice in my head shouted out wow to the mother lodes. In awe, I felt my eyebrows starting to lift for takeoff, then my eyes widened, and my mouth hung open. I was breathless. My tour guide, comfortable in his element, nonchalantly grabbed a huge diamond crystal and placed it into my hands. It would be the largest diamond I would ever hold, a diamond of two hundred carats!

"Go ahead, loupe it if you wish," he said.

Just like when I held my first gemstone at the gem show in fifth grade, I said with just as much fervor, "Oh, I wish," and that I did.

As I held that incredibly big, million-year-old diamond crystal, I thought about the journey it must have taken, crossing lands, changing from one human hand to another. Without hesitation, I raised it to the level of my eyes, turning it slowly and studying all the angles. Off in the corner of one of its shiny crystal planes, I thought I mysteriously saw someone. Startled, I shook my head. Was I seeing things or was someone really there? Examining the diamond with my loupe, I focused more carefully and saw that it was my own reflection. I was in the De Beers' diamond. I playfully searched for other reflective objects around the room, but I wished I could step back in time and see Barnato and Rhodes. However, I did spot the De Beers' diamond guide smiling, enjoying my enthusiasm, as if it reminded him of days gone by early in his career. It was then, at that moment, that I realized I too, like so many before me, had become one of the Diamond People.

All too quickly the tour came to an end. I thanked my tour guide and as we parted, he was complimentary, saying, "Anne Dale, you are as brilliant as any diamond here and I know you will bring treasure wherever you go. Good day."

Two days after my magical grand tour of De Beers, something strange happened that confirmed my Diamond People feeling. While attending an event in London, where the "best of the best" gemologists and jewelers gathered, I conversed within a circle of people until a man appeared seemingly from nowhere and approached me. Excusing himself for interrupting, he asked if I was Anne Dale, and then presented me with a first edition of the book titled *Diamond People* by A. J. Wannenburgh and Peter Johnson. After announcing it was a gift from the De Beers representative, he quickly disappeared. Someone uttered that there were only two hundred of that edition printed and only site-holders received them, which I was not. But how could the public relations officer know my thoughts, that I longed in my heart to be part of the Diamond People? That moment in time was a rite of passage. It was an invitation of trust, to be a part of the continuing, rich history of the Diamond People. It was also an opportunity to honor America and the Diamond People with hard work and perseverance.

On the cover of the book was the silhouette of world-renowned diamond cutter Gabi Tolkowsky. The book was a preliminary introduction to what would become a future friendship between the famed diamond cutter and myself. Ten years later, I finally met Gabi! His desire to share his passion and skill needed for expert diamond cutting is appreciated by all in the industry, and he firmly believes in mentoring as a way to give back to a vocation that has provided him with so much. His professional standards and respect for tradition inspire many within the jewelry trade. Diamond cutting is a unique artistic ability, a master craft that is often taught from one generation to the next. Indeed, Gabi's attitude and work ethic can be traced back to his great uncle, Marcel Tolkowsky, who was also a famous diamond cutter. Marcel was the mastermind behind the mathematical formula for the modern, round, brilliant-cut diamond, the "ideal cut" as we know it today.

Of Belgian descent, Gabi has appeared on television, in publications, and has even been spotted having tea with the Queen of England. He has been entrusted to cut many important diamonds, particularly two historically significant diamonds, one of which is the famous "Golden Jubilee." The Golden Jubilee is classified as the largest faceted diamond in the world, weighing 545.67 carats. The other famed diamond is the "Centenary," weighing 273.85 carats. The Centenary is the largest cut diamond to possess both the highest clarity diamond grade—"Flawless"—and the highest diamond color grade— "D." It is very rare to have both superior quality grades in one diamond. The Centenary has a reported insured value of $100 million.

The cutting process required so much precision that Gabi had not only a team of engineers, but also a special room built below the De Beers Diamond Research Laboratory in Johannesburg, Africa, that could maintain a specific temperature and withstand vibrations. Before he cut the Centenary, he studied it in its rough crystal form for three years. He would let the diamond speak its own language to him first. While staring into it, he collected his thoughts and planned his techniques before the first crucial cut which he cleaved by hand!

Gabi is one of the most impressive Diamond People I have met in my career. Beyond his well-deserved reputation as a famous diamond cutter, Gabi's character reflects a special romantic spirit. He is a poet, a fantastic story teller, a brilliant mathematician, and an artist who loves life with all his heart. He is respectful toward nature and life; he is quietly wise. Under his tutelage, I learned about the relationship between reflective light in a diamond and also about illuminating the human mind. He showed me that if you inspire the human spirit, great possibilities are within reach.

As I journeyed on the path of a gemologist, I continued to meet more Diamond People, gem enthusiasts, inventors, authors, scientists, and mine owners. I had the privilege to visit gem labs, jewelry manufacturers, schools, and stores. It was interesting to discover that the industry, although so vast, was also so very small, especially in light of how economically important it is to many countries.

Feeling ambitious and knowing that others in the U.S. had an interest in gemology, I formed Gem-A USA. The nonprofit organization's success was achieved with the assistance of knowledgeable people in related fields within the jewelry trade. A progressive powerhouse advisory board was formed that included national executive directors of gemological laboratories and jewelry organizations and would also include famed diamond cutter Gabi Tolkowsky. Rumors of how I, a rookie, managed to gather such an impressive board circulated. It was easy: they were authentic leaders, people who were passionate about their occupation.

Occasionally, others who managed similar business and associations believed I posed a threat to their careers. Once at a meeting in New York, I sat at a round table discussion with about seven men representing different organizations, backgrounds, nationalities, and very different goals. One man asked a question about a confidential project that I had confidential knowledge of regarding a new gem laboratory. That was not what our meeting was supposed to be about, or at least that's what I initially thought. Diamond and gem labs can bring about power and big money. However, I politely explained that for now this was not public information and could not be discussed. The conversation escalated, and heated words were exchanged between me and another man. Shockingly, he became enraged. Jumping to his feet, he lunged for my throat from across the table. Surprised, I flew to the back of my seat. Keeping my composure was very difficult in the moment; most importantly, I didn't want the men to see me cry. Thank the Good Lord the table was large, making it difficult for him to reach me. After things calmed down and the meeting was coming to a close, I excused myself to the lady's room where I called Mike and cried. "They're yelling at me and a man tried to strangle me," I said. You could have imagined what Mike thought. He stayed on the phone until I fanned my eyes dry. I would have to toughen up, just as the boys in my neighborhood taught me while growing up. I would have to learn to ignore the politics and give all my energy to the mission.

I valued every tear and every experience, for they made me a stronger person. I never took for granted the people who were kind and helpful, and I never forgot the occasional visits to De Beers Selling Organization. I learned that people who are more dedicated to the field of gemology than to themselves will be more gracious and supportive.

In a sense, I had discovered the great kahuna, believing that great possibilities were within reach, even for the little girl who grew up on Kansas Avenue.

CHAPTER 9

Traveler Meets Godzilla
Broadening Horizons

Anne in the streets of China

My childhood wishes were coming to fruition as I traveled and saw new parts of the world. I visited diamond bourses, schools, laboratories, and manufacturers. While discovering more about the world through the jewelry industry, I would also learn that international travel was not always as glamorous as I envisioned, especially when experiencing the typical inconveniences, such as delayed and canceled flights, grounded planes, airport sleepovers, detained security checks, and last-minute sprints to catch flights. On planes, I have sat with smellers, talkers, coughers, and throw-uppers. Keeping my sense of humor made travel less challenging.

My journeys would bring me across the Pacific to China. There, the government decides what will be taught, how it will be taught, and who will be doing the teaching—even outside the classroom. Colleagues warned that Chinese authorities would likely film me. Immediately after landing, we were greeted by a group of businessmen as well as a government official holding a camera who began taping. The cameraman followed us and continued filming, moving in closer and closer until he was literally about seven inches from my face.

Fatigued from the journey and having been filmed for about five hours, my mind wandered, and I escaped into my imagination. I brought myself into a scene from an old black and white movie. In my daydream, a group of Chinese men gathered in a dim, smoky room, studying secret film footage that exposed potential spies. Suddenly, I appeared on screen. I was wearing a London Fog coat and dark glasses. The glasses had mirrors attached to the inside of the frames so that I could see behind my back. In my pocket, I was carrying a secret formula that could revolutionize the jewelry industry, a formula that could instantaneously make gems grow. Unexpectedly, Godzilla showed up and ate the formula, and he quickly grew larger than ever. Delirious with jet lag, I smiled and laughed out loud. Snapping back to the reality of my stressful situation, I turned to the man with the camera and asked, "Are you filming a Godzilla movie?"

In his broken English, he responded, "Godzilla Japanese, me Chinese."

— § —

Eating from foreign menus was not always appetizing, and China's dishes proved to be the most interesting. My first taste of Chinese cuisine was "Drunken Shrimp," which consisted of live shrimp that swam around in a large bowl of beer. As I watched the shrimp swim about, I too felt my insides swimming. As the group of Chinese men gathered their chopsticks, plucking away at the moving tailed shrimp, they tried desperately to convince me that this was not only fun but tasty. Then it was on to the delicacies, such as the ball of a camel's foot along with a few crunchy duck feet. Some foods I simply would not eat—live scorpions or skinned rat on a stick in the markets. Sitting down for a meal could be an adventure, like the time a waiter rolled a live duck in on a cart. Everyone smiled, anticipating its tasty, juicy meat. The grinning server was delighted to have the opportunity to cut away. Chop! The duck's head came off, and then the belly was sliced open and out came the prize, the delicacy: the heart. After the performance, it was revealed that the guest of honor was to receive the special morsel. The special guest was me. I was strongly encouraged to stand and accept such an honor. As I tried to convince myself that the old cliché "mind-over-matter" was true, I turned several shades of green. I dared not chew, so I swallowed the heart whole and took a big gulp of some Chinese beer. Soon, "Could I have some more beer?" became a common phrase of mine while dining out overseas.

— § —

Americans value certain commodities differently than individuals in other countries. Interestingly, although China produces various types of paper products for worldwide use, I found it to be lacking in some of their own cities. Was it considered very valuable? School textbooks were printed on very fine paper, similar to American tracing paper. In some cities, children wore no diapers and their bottoms were exposed, ready to fire if the need arose. Toilet paper was limited in some areas. I remember watching a few women sneak into a nice office building in a more Westernized city simply to steal a handful of toilet paper.

During a break in a business meeting in an increasingly modern city in China, I asked a female hostess the unthinkable. Knowing that in many places a hole in the floor serves as a toilet—a facility I was not eager to master—I asked, "Is there toilet paper in the lady's room?" My request resulted in a huge production; they had to retrieve the special lady who had the key to the exclusive toilet paper vault. Hearing her echoing, firm heels walk down a long hallway toward me, I was soon greeted by her unwelcoming presence and stoic, unsmiling face. I had come to the conclusion that I, the American, had created a quandary. With a strong, quick, and curt Chinese accent, she asked, "What do you need?"

As I desperately tried to tell her not to worry about it, that it really was no big deal, my Chinese hostess, who wanted me to feel welcome, kept repeating, "She want toilet paper, she want toilet paper, she want toilet paper."

The special toilet paper lady then pulled out a massive keychain from under her many layers of clothing, as if the keys were chained around her body. She instructed me to wait. Ten minutes later, I heard those same echoing sounds of her heels come down that long hallway again—but I didn't see any toilet paper. As she got closer to me, she opened her palm and revealed two small 3" x 5" inch squares of paper. I picked each up by its delicate, fragile corner, said thank you, and we bowed.

— § —

I was with a group of gemologists heading to a Chinese government building for a meeting, and I was the only woman in the car. As we approached the building, there were men with machine guns surrounding and patrolling the area. Intimidated by the reality of such a scene, my jetlagged eyes widened and my heart palpitated. I was sitting behind the driver. The driver stopped at a checkpoint, and I was told to put my window down so the armed men could get a clear look at my face. One of the men leaned over into the window and came within inches of my nose. His searing gaze matched his aggressive foreign tone. The driver responded in Chinese; I could only trust that he was speaking on my behalf and doing a convincing job. Every time I heard the driver say my name, I nodded with confidence as if I understood everything they said. He continued to stare at me while remaining in my space; I assumed it was to intimidate me, and it was working. Everyone remained quiet. I was confused as to what was happening. The guard asked to see my passport. Then he asked me to write my name on a piece of paper. He motioned for us to drive through. As we drove away, the driver explained, "I told the guard you were a famous movie star in America. He wanted your autograph."

We all laughed.

— § —

My journeys brought me across the Atlantic to Europe, allowing me to become acquainted with people of other cultures and faiths. While waiting in line at an airport, a panic-faced woman from Tel Aviv turned to me, paused, and then soaked my clothes with projectile vomit. I tried to catch her as she collapsed to the floor. Coming to, she tried desperately to communicate, asking me if I were Jewish. Nervously shaking my head no, I found myself speaking loud and slow, as if that would break through our language barrier. I kept telling her everything will be fine: "Jesus will help you; let us pray together." Signing the cross, I began, "In the name of the Father, the Son, and the Holy Spirit . . ." A colleague traveling with me looked at me as if I had lost my mind. He said, "She's Jewish," questioning my faith-based approach. "You're going to give her a heart attack if she hasn't had one already." Feeling sympathetic to the lady's situation, not realizing my gaffe, I responded with, "Oh my," and then asked, "Would you like to hold my rosary?" Looking into her eyes I don't think she minded, because we were one-in-the-same, just people in transit.

— § —

But if you travel enough, odds are that you will eventually be observed by transit onlookers too. Never to be forgotten, I was on a flight that just got off the ground. Suddenly, I was struck by a very ill feeling; something I ate for lunch didn't agree with me. I waited for an unoccupied lavatory that never came to be. Wanting some privacy, I ran to the back of the plane to find a place where I could throw my guts up. There, I quickly hugged a tall garbage can. My spewing sounds could be heard down the aisle, and I was on view for anyone to watch if they wanted. As I broke a sweat, I looked up and there stood a small child taking my picture opposite a squeamish flight attendant in a state of fright with his body pinned up against the nearby wall.

— § —

Humility boosts character. Post 9-11, while grabbing my bags from a luggage carousel in an international airport, I was asked, "Excuse me, may I see your passport?"

There stood a military soldier with a machine gun and German shepherd by his side. I handed him my passport, and he asked, "Are you here for business or pleasure?"

Wanting to be honest, I answered, "Business."

"What is your business?"

As I explained, he interrupted me and requested to search my luggage. He instructed me to open my bag on the floor and step away from it. Another soldier came over to inspect it with some sort of stick-like object. It was as if he had a strong need to create a whirlpool by stirring the contents of my suitcase, exposing my under garments. There I stood, an American southern girl, sharing my underwear with the world. Mama would have been mortified.

— § —

Being female posed other challenges as well. Not only is the jewelry industry mostly maintained by men, but so are large purchases at a diamond bourse. A bourse is an essential place where structured commerce of diamond trading and purchasing transpires. Available to a buyer are numerous diamond parcels, from small matched melee to exceptionally gorgeous big diamonds of every shape, size, color, and clarity. Depending on the location of the country, a diamond bourse and manufacturing facility will have its own unique procedures and language for business. Many of their long lasting business relationships are built on years of trust and tradition. For some, a handshake seals a deal worth millions of dollars. With other bourses, it can strongly be implied that a buyer must indulge in spending a certain amount annually or he may not be welcomed back to buy. Obviously, such places are well-guarded as security is essential. Some have barbwire fences, bullet-proof glass, cameras that record everything both inside and outside the premises, armed men with machine guns, armored cars, and trained security dogs. Some bourses install concrete poles that surround the premises and rise from the ground at the push of a button. The poles prevent vehicles from entering or exiting the area. They also have armed, intimidating check points. They are not there for tourists, information, or to be photographed. With their stern faces, the guards watch and wait for any suspicious movement.

Some diamond bourses require that their security agents hold your passport before you are allowed to enter. On one occasion, I was the only American female among thirty men waiting in a security line to get into a bourse. An officer called me to come forward. Hesitant, I turned my head, pretending I didn't see him, or hoping that he had called the man waiting behind me. As I continued to look away, he yelled to me again, this time louder than before. Being female, I was terrified, thinking the worst. Would I be harassed, ridiculed, or physically searched, privately or publicly? I walked to the front of the line. With a heartless face, the officer looked into my eyes for a few seemingly long seconds, took my passport, and motioned for me to pass through. The uncertainty as to why he did this raced through my mind. Relieved and glad to move on, I quickly shuffled onto a crowded elevator filled with men. Suddenly, everyone became silent and all conversations ceased in the elevator. One man, putting his hand out, stopped the doors from closing. I was not welcome. The faces in the elevator glared at me with repugnance, appalled by my gender. Most of the men vacated the elevator, refusing to share their space with a woman. As the air cleared, I inhaled and regained focus on my journey among the Diamond People. An experienced colleague confirmed my suspicion: I was a political pawn. The reason I was plucked from line and given express service was to deliver a pointed message to this group of international guests, that a woman was going to be prioritized over them even though they were men. And then when I jumped into the elevator, I was met with more gender discrimination and was dismissed as inferior by the same group of foreigners. Funny, women wear more jewelry than men.

— § —

Matters more serious than prejudices can be experienced when buying internationally, such as intimidating policing. I was filming an educational video on diamonds near a bourse. As the cameraman organized the officially-approved government papers, he explained that I needed to recite my lines in one take, no mistakes, because the government authorization did not matter to bourse security. "As soon as I remove the camera from my bag, security will be on their way to shut us down and may threaten to arrest us. Do it quickly and correctly," he instructed.

It was a dreary, cold day. He clipped a small mic to my shirt. Barely having enough time to take off my coat, he called, "Action!" My nerves formed a lump in my throat. I forced down a dry swallow before I walked toward the camera and recited my lines. He was right. Armored cars raced toward us, and security poles emerged from the ground below. During the filming, I tried to remain calm, smile, and say all that I needed to say without sounding cold, rushed, or terrified. I don't know how, but miraculously, we pulled it off in the one take. At the orders of security, the cameraman put his camera down and showed the necessary papers and our passports. Other armed officers stood a few feet away with loaded guns and leashed dogs in hand, ready for action. As the cameraman tried to explain, the armed security radioed in our names. Good news: we were simply told to leave the area immediately and were escorted from the premises.

— § —

For the most part, I felt welcome in most foreign countries as foreigners practiced their English with me or curiously petted my head to feel the texture of my hair and skin. However, there were some people I met who presented uncomfortable challenges and insults to my nationality.

I was in Europe on business and had a tight schedule—France for one day and an early morning meeting in Belgium the following day. In order to make the Belgium meeting, I had to catch the last scheduled train out of France. As I stood in line waiting for a taxi, it started to rain. There was no shelter and no offers to share an umbrella, not toward me, an American. After standing for about twenty minutes in the pouring rain, an elderly couple with an umbrella waddled up to the line. As they eyed the length of the line, they stopped to give me, the American, their look of disfavor, and then proceeded to step right in front of me—something we call in America "cutting" the line. Indoctrinated with certain beliefs by my family, I was taught to be respectful of older people. However, traffic was increasing, and I was concerned about making that last train. I pointed to the back of the line to show them where it ended and where they should go to wait their turn. They really didn't care and continued to give me rude and condescending looks, as if my American presence was offending them. Surprised by their behavior, I repeated my motions a few more times, but they purposely ignored me and remained in their "cut" position. The other French people waiting in line began shouting at the elderly couple to move to the end. The couple still would not budge. So when it was my turn to get into the next taxi, I assertively stepped in front of them and placed my hand on the handle of the cab door. Shockingly, the old man slapped my arm hard, threatening me to move. Determined to get into the taxi, I accepted his challenge. To my surprise, the old man turned out to be stronger than I thought. As he pushed me down to the ground, he yelled at me in French. The only words I understood were "Stupid American." The old woman joined in on the fight, raising her purse in the air, trying to smack me on the head. If I had any doubts of their intentions, or thoughts that they were "just old," I quickly ditched them. It became very clear that they knew exactly what they were doing when they began to spit in my direction. My tolerance level had peaked, and I went into automatic survival mode. While I protected my head from her purse with my forearm, I let out a loud roar as if I was crazy. Jumping up, I elbowed the man as if he were a linebacker, clearing the way to the taxi door. Grabbing the handle, I turned toward the woman and gave her one of my tough red, white, and blue looks. I meant business. By this time, the cab driver had jumped out and started screaming. Others who had been waiting for a cab yelled back at the taxi driver. It was a frenzy of about a dozen people shouting in the street. With mascara streaming down my cold, rain-washed face and my hair plastered to my head, I proudly raised my chin, pointed to my chest, and proclaimed, "I am an American!" The elderly couple, stunned by my boldness, backed down. The spectators who were entertained by the feuding began to applaud, cheering me on, smiling, and shouting cheers of "Yay American!"

After I got into the cab, I had a spontaneous need to restore my American dignity. Smiling, I stuck my head out of the window as we drove off and loudly began singing the "Star Spangled Banner." That was a profound moment for me. Upon foreign soil, I proudly professed my nationality with conviction before strangers, a defining moment of who I am, and where my heart and my home are. Even when my nationality is not always respected in other countries, I am, and will always remain, as much a part of America as America is a part of me.

— § —

It's strange that the world can be so big, yet so small. I learned that the human spirit in business is shared everywhere, expressed in smiles, handshakes, nods, hugs, and laughter. Although "my horizons were broadening," I learned that the further I was from home-base, the less control I had. I wasn't on Kansas Avenue anymore. I questioned how far I really wanted to journey. There was no place like home—our American way of life is special.

CHAPTER 10

The Jeweler's Shop

A Time and A Season

Anne in jewelry store

The dream Mike and I shared together was back home —our jewelry shop. It was the place in my heart I longed to be. I missed the one-on-one experiences with the customers and the everyday excitement of a jewelry store.

When customers visit the store, they usually bring two important things with them: their emotions and their stories. All of which revolve around the jewelry pieces they own, lost, or imagine. Customers come from all walks of life; they are the rich, poor, upright, young, and old. Some come because of the past and some for the future. Some are in love or want to be loved. I journey with my customers in their dreams and in their rites of passage, sharing with them their most precious gifts which are the people and things that occupy their hearts. Customers are like an extended family. I feel privileged to celebrate some of their life's joys: births, baptisms, engagements, anniversaries, birthdays, graduations, employment, retirement, and occasionally my favorite reason—just because. At times, I am also part of their tragedies: divorces and deaths.

Owning a jewelry store is unlike any other business. It differs in that it does not sell products that fill needs, such as groceries, clothing, or automobiles. A day in the life of a jeweler is far more exciting; it celebrates the human heart and relationships motivated by love.

Customers buy jewelry based on an emotional connection. As a jeweler, I act as a conduit for my customer, creating the ideal jewelry piece that symbolizes and satisfies their emotional expectations. One of the most traditional, yet challenging of these experiences is finding the perfect engagement ring. The mere presentation of an engagement ring has to convey a heart's desire.

For a woman, her engagement ring represents the commitment of a man's intent to love her forever. It is a treasure that she will admire and wear all the days of her life. It means even more to her than just the pretty bling. It captures a hopeful heart and an exchange of future promises as a couple dreams together. We ladies can thank Archduke Maximilian of Austria for the celebratory tradition of engagement rings. It is believed that his lady, Mary of Burgundy, was the first to receive a diamond engagement ring on August 17th, 1477. He placed it on the third finger of her left hand because it was thought that the vein of love, "vene amoris," flowed from that finger and traveled straight to the heart.

Emotions run high in the jewelry store as customers engage in conversations with other customers, ask questions, form opinions, or share their stories.

The following stories are musings based upon customers' interactions...

SWEPT AWAY

It is not uncommon for a customer who has been married for a while to eavesdrop on a young couple while they shop for an engagement ring.

One day two customers, a young man and an older woman, were standing next to each other at the jewelry counter, both picking up their custom-made jewelry. The young man, soon to be engaged, was picking up a diamond engagement ring, and the woman was picking up a special piece for her husband, commemorating forty-five years of marriage. As the woman glanced over to his engagement ring, and he in turn glanced at her purchase, they both acknowledged the anticipation of their gift-giving with a conspiratorial smile.

"It goes by so quickly . . . May I see the ring?" she asked.

"Sure . . . Do you like it?" he asked.

"Oh, it is stunning!"

"I couldn't make up my mind whether to give her a round or a princess cut diamond. I really hope she likes it. I still don't know how I am going to propose," he replied.

"May I share a story with you about when my Harry proposed to me?"

Hoping for an idea, he said, "Sure."

"Well, I love to dance. However, when I met Harry, who was somewhat reserved, he didn't care to dance. Truth was he didn't know how, nor did he want to learn. But knowing that I did, he would take me to the town hall dances, the happening place to be on the weekends. Even though I danced with my friends, it just wasn't the same. I really wanted to dance with Harry. After dating for several months, he phoned one evening and suggested that I dress extra special for that night's dance. He said he had a surprise and that I would have to meet him at the dance. Anticipating the surprise, I wore my favorite green dress. When I arrived, I scanned the crowd and spotted him. He was dressed in a suit and tie, his hair perfectly combed and looking so handsome. To my surprise,

Harry asked me to dance. You see, he had been taking lessons in secret. We danced and danced. I couldn't have been happier. When one of our favorite songs ended, Harry went up onto the stage and stood behind the band's microphone. I didn't know what to think. I could see he was nervous. After clearing his throat, he said, "May I have everyone's attention?" He paused, looking out into the crowd. "Especially yours, Sarah?" he asked. This was not an easy thing for Harry due to his modest temperament. Pulling out a piece of paper from his back pocket, he began to read:

> *Sarah, you are the reason I breathe.*
> *You are the reason I look forward to every day of my life.*
> *You make me complete.*
> *I can't imagine life without you.*
> *Sarah, will you marry me?*

"Shocked and in love, of course I said 'Yes.' He hopped off the stage, walked through the crowd, and came straight toward me. He dropped on one knee and put his hand in his coat pocket. I then heard him whisper under his breath, "The ring?" He started to panic when he realized the engagement ring was not there. He stood up frantically searching all of his pockets for the ring. Filled with emotion, I threw my arms around him and whispered in his ear, 'It's not the ring but you I want to marry.' At that moment, his friend came running up with a ring box in hand. He had forgotten that he had asked his friend to hold it while we danced.

"So relax. If you two are in love, your proposal and the ring will be everything that you dreamed it to be. I am sure of it."

— § —

Not all stories are that picturesque. Every once in a while a couple visits the jewelry shop looking for the perfect engagement ring, bringing with them a false sense of love. Some believe by becoming engaged they will fix or boost their feelings for one another. However, some men put off engagements, afraid of commitment, while some women are only infatuated with bride attention, the bells and whistles of a wedding party. I refer to those women as Phantom Bridezillas. They're in love with the trimmings of planning a wedding—not the groom-to-be. Phantom Bridezilla dreams about her day and only her day, placing high, unreal expectations on the groom. When a bride-to-be becomes too focused on the details of what her ring should look like and what size her diamond should be—not taking into account the groom's financial situation—they should not marry. Usually in these types of relationships, there are trust issues, selfishness, and incredible insecurity towards others' perceptions.

Once, a young man who hoped for more than he could afford placed a one-carat diamond engagement ring on layaway. Anxious to give the ring to his future fiancée, he borrowed money from not only his parents but also a buddy and a finance company. This was not a good sign. Only a few days after taking the engagement ring out of layaway, he returned to the store with his future bride-to-be. Wanting to meet his bride, I greeted them with, "Well, hello."

"Hey, Mrs. Anne."

I could tell by his facial expression that he was feeling uncomfortable. Awkwardly, he said, "I need to return the ring . . . we were thinking a bigger diamond."

She was beautiful, picture perfect. Every hair was in place, her handbag matched her shoes, and she even had glued-on sparkles to decorate her fingernails.

Suspecting a Phantom Bridezilla, I confirmed my own suspicions as she spoke the cruel words, "The diamond is just too small for my hands. I need something bigger, at least two carats."

I knew the young man could not afford to spend any more money. Hoping that perhaps I read her wrong, I began with, "No problem, we want you both to be happy." Holding the ring in hand

I began to examine the soon-to-be-returned diamond with my jewelers' loupe. "This diamond is very special. It formed over a million years ago, fashioned to perfection for this moment in time. The diamond cutter cut it so that light could travel through it at an incredible speed of about 77,000 miles per second. Uniquely beautiful, its attributes make it one-of-a-kind. Please have a seat by the diamond case."

As we sat, I continued. "You should have seen how he carefully took his time studying many diamonds before this one captured his heart. Over and over, he kept going back to the one he picked for you, stating that the diamond was as beautiful as you. Did you know a miner has to collect about a million pieces of rough material before a cutter can yield a faceted and polished one-carat diamond? And, a good diamond cutter knows that in order to capture the maximum brilliance of a diamond, he will usually need to remove 40 to 60 percent of the rough material before completion." I wanted to give her an opportunity to understand that a one-carat diamond engagement ring is just as special as a two-carat. "Would you like to see those attributes he saw?"

Without any interest, she immediately responded, "No, thanks. It's just too small. What's the biggest diamond you've got?"

Feeling sorry for the young man, I couldn't help myself. I did something I rarely do. I pretended I wanted to talk price with him, pulling him over to a corner. Looking him in the eye like the designated matchmaker of a town, I whispered, "I have waited on many couples and sold many engagement rings, and this one is not meant to be. This is not the way it is supposed to be. I'm going to tell you something you don't want to hear: don't marry this girl. The price you will pay will be a greater sacrifice than any debt you will incur."

Looking down, he said, "Come on, Mrs. Anne. She's alright. I'll get the money together somehow."

I took it a step further.

"Don't you have any pride left in you, or has she spent that too? Don't be her stepping stone . . . You have been blinded by the Phantom Bridezilla."

"The what?" he asked.

"The Phantom Bridezilla! It hides behind all her lipstick. It is selfish, and it will take you for everything until you've got nothing left to give."

But he insisted, "No, Mrs. Anne, don't worry about me. I will be all right. She just has long fingers."

Even though I felt disgusted with the situation, I did what he wanted me to do: I waited on her, listening to her giggle here and giggle there. She tried on just about every diamond engagement ring in the store. I could see beads of sweat begin to form on his forehead and his mouth became dry as he swallowed every time he read a higher price tag. He stood there quiet as a mouse. The price he would pay was more than any tag he read. In the end, he gave in, and she got what she wanted. She had conquered, and on layaway went a new and bigger diamond. Somehow he got the needed money.

Six months after he married her, he came into the store with his head and heart hanging even lower than before. He wanted to know if she had come by to try and sell the ring back.

"You were right. I was blinded by the Phantom Bride thing. I had to declare bankruptcy."

"I am so sorry. Wait, don't leave. I have something I want to give you. You know, you're not the first to be taken by the Phantom Bridezilla—nor will you be the last."

I placed in his hand a small pouch that held in it a beautiful, sparkling gemstone.

"What's this?" he asked.

"I want you to keep it as a reminder that a gem of a girl will never use you as a stepping stone again. You will know when you find her because she will give her heart to you as much as you desire to give her yours."

He thanked me and placed the pouch in his pocket. Three years later, he came back into the store. I hardly recognized him at first. He smiled, reflecting wisdom and confidence. He told me he was getting engaged, but this time she's a gem.

"I need to buy a new engagement ring."

He pulled the pouch out of his pocket that contained the gemstone I had given him years ago.

"You think we can incorporate this?

— § —

When a heart is full of love, it is capable of giving the best gifts, which are sometimes measured by the sacrifice of the gift giver.

It was a week before Christmas, and business was good. A man in his early twenties came into the store. I noticed that something about his walk was different; there was something insecure or gentle about him. His hair was a soft brown, and he wore a nervous smile. I asked if I could help him. He stuttered, "I'm, I'm, I'm looking for a wedding ring."

I walked him over to the case of wedding rings where I showed him a few bands.

"Do you have any with a diamond set on top of the ring?" he asked.

"Sure, are you getting married?" I asked.

"No, I'm already married. I just never could afford a diamond engagement ring, and I wanted to get my wife one for a Christmas present."

"How long have you been married?" I asked.

"Three, three years," he replied.

I needed him to reveal his budget, so I tried to break the ice by engaging in small talk. Eventually, I asked, "How much money were you hoping to spend?"

"I have two hundred dollars," he said.

I thought to myself, this poor guy has no clue as to the cost of a diamond wedding set. He was genuinely real—no act. Trying hard not to burst his bubble, I said, "Let me show you what you can buy near that price range." I showed him some small diamond promise rings.

Disappointed, he released a drawn out, "Ohhhh." Then he paused, and with a disheartened and accepting tone he said, "I guess I'm gonna have to find a job and save some money."

I mentioned our layaway plan, but he politely shook his head no. His heart was set on buying her a ring for Christmas.

Throughout my years in sales and of all the people I have waited on, this guy was just different. I was touched by his innocence. I admired his thoughtfulness and the childlike love he possessed. It was as if he had a fleet of angels surrounding him, inspiring me to be gracious. I felt compelled to go above and beyond to assist him.

Since my heart was moved and business was good, I thought I would give back to someone who could use it. It was a chapter in his life that I wanted to be part of, making this one of the most memorable Christmases for him and his wife. I removed three diamond bridal sets from the jewelry case, each of which contained both a beautiful diamond engagement ring plus a wedding band costing more than his budget. As he stared at the rings, I said to him, "Choose one for your wife."

With a puzzled look he said, "But all I have is two hundred dollars."

"I realize that. This is my Christmas gift to you."

His eyes were filled with amazement and gratitude; you would have thought he saw a stream of fireworks light up a dark night sky. "Really, are you sure?" he asked.

"Yes, I am sure."

I felt the true meaning of the words "Merry Christmas." He

chose one of the bridal sets, and I giftwrapped it for him. He thanked me several times. Afterward, some of the employees made comments that he was a con artist who had taken advantage of me, but in my heart I refused to believe that.

Christmas morning came, and as I watched my children open their gifts, I thought about him. In my imagination I envisioned the look on his wife's face as she opened the ring box. Quietly smiling to myself, I got back to the gift giving in my own home.

Two weeks after Christmas, a lady came into the store asking for me.

"I just want to say thank you. My brother came into your store right before Christmas to buy a diamond ring for his wife. He only had two hundred dollars to spend."

She continued, "You see, my brother was injured in a terrible accident, and he has some limitations that have affected his ability to work. He and his wife live next door to me so that I can help them out. His wife works ... but they really, really, don't have much. He sold his TV so he could buy her a diamond ring for Christmas. That's how he got the two hundred dollars to spend. Now they come over to my house every day to watch TV. My brother hasn't stopped talking about the real nice lady at the jewelry store. His wife loves the ring. You made their Christmas. My brother's birthday is coming up and the family is chipping in to buy him a TV."

Hearing this man's experience profoundly influenced me. The size of his sacrifice was not near the size of his heart.

— § —

Men sometimes find it more difficult than women to express emotion. Jewelry is one invaluable way to bridge the gap. However, some men hesitate to purchase jewelry because they are financially tight, possessing an overbearing "A" type personality that tries to justify a purchase based on rationalizations. Some are terrified to make the wrong decision, and some are searching desperately for appreciation from their eternally unhappy women who frequently return their gifts. But for most women, jewelry purchases from their man can mean the world to them.

Into the store walked a woman in her fifties. Her appearance and body language were humble, as one who gives of herself and expects nothing in return. She stood quietly waiting for me to admire the beautiful diamond pendant she was wearing. I could see joy bursting in her eyes. I looked at it and immediately recognized that it was one of my designs. Proudly, she touched her pendant. She told me how it was the first piece of jewelry that her husband had bought for her in thirty years. She spoke casual words of gratitude, but what I heard was how her husband was her knight in shining armor. Lucky for him, his thirty years of marriage to a patient woman paid off in that one piece of jewelry.

— § —

The layout of the jewelry store is an elongated, oval-shaped island of cases. Too many times I watch women float around the island on a hope boat, wishing and dreaming that their significant others will buy an intimate, special piece. If he hasn't bought them jewelry in the past fifteen years, chances are he probably never will. My advice to those women is to dock the hope boat and buy it themselves.

I love to wait on appreciative men who have been maturely married for many years. Their wisdom in knowing that life passes quickly, along with being grateful for their spouse, is demonstrated by their desire to make their wives happy. But for some, as life's clock moves quickly with each passing day, the regret of putting off expressing one's love and appreciation may arrive when it is too late.

I remember this one man who walked anxiously into the store. Although his mission was serious, his mind was occupied with something else. Unsettled, he paced around the island. When he stopped to look at the jewelry, it seemed the only thing he saw was his reflection on top of the glass jewelry cases.

I asked, "Can I help you?"

"I don't know what I am looking for. Maybe you can suggest something. I want to buy my wife something very special. I was thinking maybe pearls. I really haven't bought her much jewelry in the past. In fact, I haven't bought her much at all."

I showed him the various strands of pearls, explaining why they are priced differently and about their value. He could care less; his mind wandered in another world. As I spoke he just watched my lips move as if I was Charlie Brown's teacher. So I just stopped.

"Tell me about your wife," I said.

"Well she is about this tall, and her hair is . . ." His eyes filled, and tears began to stream down his face. His secret was revealed.

"My wife wants to leave me, she wants to divorce me. I don't know why. I don't know why she wants to leave me. We've been married for twenty-two years. We have two beautiful children. I don't know what to do."

He broke down and cried. I went around the jewelry case and put my arm around the man. I handed him some tissue, and he wiped his face. "She says I never buy her anything. I never take her out . . . just give me those," he said, pointing to a strand of pearls.

My hunch was that he had lost that emotional connection with his wife. The only thing I could offer him was a tissue, beautiful jewelry wrapped in a box, and a prayer.

As he watched me wrap the pearls, he asked, "Do you think it will work?" as if I had a crystal ball to see into the past twenty-two years of their marriage or into their future. Whatever his marital problems were, his timing was more than likely too late. On the other hand, here he was trying, trying to make things right. As I listened to what he shared, it seemed he had neglected giving his wife any intimate attention for years. In my retail store, I've waited on many married women. Wives want their husbands to know that they are more than the laundry lady, the cook, or the one who holds the house together. They long for their husbands to look into their eyes and see the spark that drew them together in the first place.

One year later, he returned to my store. "Do you remember me?" he asked. "I am the guy whose marriage was in bad shape. I broke down in your store. I bought a strand of pearls."

"Yes, yes, I remember. How are you? What happened? Did the pearls work?" I asked.

"No and yes . . . she divorced me, and now we are dating again. I would like to buy her something. You could say I have a hot date with her this weekend. I never want to lose her again."

Reunited and now a regular customer, he buys mostly under the sway of "Just Because I Love You."

— § —

Not all spousal jewelry purchases are from the heart. When a wife returns a husband's jewelry purchase for a "refund," it's a red flag indicating that there is a problem in the relationship. It is rarely about the jewelry. If it is not her style, surely she can find something else to her liking. If it doesn't fit, it can be adjusted. When these women come into the store, they either come in without saying much or they say a lot.

One day, a woman came into the store to return a beautiful diamond bracelet for a cash refund. Initially, she stated that it just didn't fit, that it was too big. I offered to adjust it. Then she stated that she just didn't like the style of the bracelet. I offered to show her other bracelets. And before long, it came out: "My husband is having an affair, and it's the second time I've caught him."

Expressing my sympathy, I asked her how long they had been married and if they had children. Angrily, she replied, "Seventeen years and three children."

After she shed a few tears, I had an idea. "Does your husband get along with his mother-in-law? You know, with your mother?"

"No, not really. He tells me I act like her whenever I question him," she replied.

"May I make a suggestion?" I asked.

She wiped away her tears and running mascara. "Sure."

Delicately, with a soft, slow projection of my voice, I suggested, "Why don't you give that diamond bracelet to his mother-in-law and make sure she thanks him for it. It won't fix your marriage, but it may offer a moment of satisfaction."

Liking the idea, she smiled.

"Would you gift wrap it for me?" she asked.

— § —

Tragedies such as death sometimes send customers to our shop as well, but not all situations can be treated the same. Each person handles death in his or her own way.

A widow's husband's death called her back to visit her homeland, Italy. With some of the inherited money from his life insurance policy, she wanted to purchase jewelry gifts for their children and for some of the family members she would visit in Italy. While walking around the store trying to decide what to purchase, she opened her purse and pulled out a framed 8" x 10" portrait of her deceased husband. She placed his picture on the jewelry counter so he could be part of her shopping experience. As she went about the store, she smiled and spoke to him, asking, "Dominick, do you like?" As I watched her, I was impressed with how much she loved him and her unique way of handling her grief.

— § —

My great aunt's passing—my first experience with death—occurred when I was just twelve years old. The pain of this loss has always stayed with me, and so has the memory of her beautiful wristwatch.

My great aunt was my namesake, so naturally I studied things about her. From my adolescent perspective, I thought my Great

Aunt Annie's advanced age meant we didn't have much in common. Occasionally, I would go to her house in the French Quarter for lunch or dinner. The home was a traditional framed, raised, shotgun house which is a common style in that part of New Orleans. Everything in her house was immaculate. I also remember that it was in that house that I was required to eat split pea soup for the first time. I had never seen such an intense green liquid in all my childhood years. I hated peas. I would hold my breath and swallow while trying to think of other things. With every spoonful, I thought I was going to throw up. In slow motion, I spooned in that green liquid while staring at my great aunt's missing teeth and the milky white, dry, and wrinkled skin of her arms. The only thing that got me through such torture was to shift my concentration to her beautiful diamond watch that I admired. Focusing on it intently, I watched the second hand sweep slowly, and I would count the diamonds that surrounded the face. That watch got me through a lot of soup.

She passed, and at her wake I experienced the sadness of death. Disturbing as this may sound to some, one of my father's Italian family's customs was to kiss the deceased on the forehead before the casket was closed as a display of a final respect. Today, I am sure many psychologists would find such a tradition disturbing, but for me and the family, it was customary. The strange kiss experience was particularly chilling, but I gained a real understanding of what's behind the concept. As I looked at her body resting peacefully in the casket, the last thing that I noticed was her watch, the watch that told me things about her character and how she defined herself as a person. She had worn it for years, looking at it every day of her life. Her watch had become a part of her, thus giving me a future insight as to the value people place on their jewelry.

— § —

Death is hard, but it's even harder when children die. Here is the sad story of a death too close to home, never to be forgotten. It was the first day of the school year, and I was bringing my kids to class. My children were excited. Backing out of the driveway, I realized I had forgotten my purse. Pulling back in, I hurried into the house to grab it. We set out again, still with the same enthusiasm. I spent those few seconds smiling, watching my children in the rearview mirror. As I approached the traffic light to exit out of our subdivision, I waited behind three cars. Suddenly, a car flew out of control and became airborne. What happened next felt surreal. Within seconds, it crashed into the first car that was ahead of me. Then, everything grew silent. In shock, I just froze; I couldn't move. I was trying to process what had just happened. The people in the other two cars got out to see if they could help. "Get to a phone" came to mind. I backed up and turned around, racing madly back home to get to a phone to call the police (this was in the days before cell phones). I was overcome by the realization that if I had not gone back to get my purse, those seconds of horrific tragedy could have easily belonged to my family.

Three people died in that accident. Days later, I received a phone call at the jewelry store. The call was about the jewelry that the victims were wearing at the time of their death. It was a request to clean and straighten the jewelry so that they could be dressed with it for the wake. When the jewelry was brought to the shop, it was placed in my hands with traces of blood. Disturbing thoughts ran through my mind. I tried hard not to imagine the impact, but found myself staring at the crushed jewelry. As I placed the jewelry in an ultrasonic cleaner, Mike and I watched the blood dissolve in the water. With a heavy heart and flowing tears, we reshaped and polished the jewelry with great care. It would be one of the most important jewelry repair jobs Mike and I would encounter in our shop.

— § —

Even when death's sting grazes us slightly, it leaves a permanent mark that can change a person for life.

A young man in his teens came into the shop. He handed me a gold crucifix pendant that was broken in half.

"Wow, what happened to this crucifix?" I asked.

He told me he had been in a very bad automobile accident. He began to tell his story but was a little uncertain about sharing his newly found faith in God; it didn't take long for him to warm up.

His story was of an event that would change him forever.

"Well . . . well, you see I was driving on the highway at night, about 10:00 pm. I was heading back home from my girlfriend's house. I was jamming out to my music, and no, I wasn't drinking. It was weird because I was thinking about my girlfriend, my new job, how I will be graduating from high school this year, that sort of stuff, when all of a sudden, a truck swerved over into my lane and headed straight for me. It all happened so quickly. All I saw were these big, bright headlights coming toward me. He nailed me straight on. My car and his truck were smashed—I mean totaled. I blacked out. I don't know for how long. My chest was pinned behind the steering wheel. Paramedics had to cut me out of the car. I could hear them talking, but I couldn't move. When the impact happened, my necklace broke, cutting the crucifix right in half. It was as if it was a shield between me and the steering wheel, between life and death. It was a miracle. It stopped the steering wheel from crushing my chest. The paramedics couldn't believe my lungs didn't collapse and that I was alive. The other half of the cross fell in my lap. The paramedic gave it to me to hold while in the ambulance. He said, 'You're a miracle, kid. You've been given a second chance in life.'

"I know this may sound strange, but I believe God used my crucifix to protect me. It's really special to me. I need you to fix it, and it doesn't matter if it looks like it has been repaired. I just need it. I'm so glad to be alive."

His crucifix would remind him of his close encounter with death, and more importantly, to appreciate the gift of life.

Sometimes faith alone is the only preparation for a blindsiding storm in life.

CHAPTER 11

KATRINA

A Storm

Hurricane Katrina aftermath, 2005

R eminiscing had to come to an end; I would have to set aside recounting stories about jewelry and my journeys as a gemologist—Katrina was approaching. The electricity going out was just the beginning of her effects. Without discrimination, her winds would come to change the lives of rich, poor, old, young, white, and black. She was not to be underestimated.

With the anticipation of Katrina's arrival, emotions were escalating among everyone in the house. Katrina could be compared to the worst imaginable uninvited house guest: destructive, loud, and unpredictable. Our unexpected house guest was making the kids louder and more rambunctious, encouraging the smokers to smoke more cigarettes, and worse, wearing on the patience of the hostess.

Katrina's strengthening winds sounded like a whale bellowing. As I peeked through the taped and boarded windows, it was impossible to confirm which direction the gusts were throwing their punches. Whipped around by the wind, the rain was darting north and south one minute, then to the east and west the next. My eyes were trying to recognize some semblance of consistency in the wind pattern.

I noticed that the utility door was now swelling from the dampness, becoming very difficult to shut. Within minutes, two inches of water accumulated near the door. I yelled at the kids, "No more running. Inside voices only!" To the smokers: "Don't open the door, and no more smoking!"

The fact that I felt responsible for the safety of everyone in our home had become an alarming reality. I was fixated on trying to identify any threatening noises. A pressurizing sound was coming from one of the taped windows. The glass panes were bowing and vibrating. Fearing that the window would fling shards of glass about the room, I stuffed it with a blanket. Mike ran outside into the rain to reinforce the window with more wood. Each time the wind would howl, I tried desperately to differentiate every sound, asking myself fretful questions: "What was that: tornado or tree?"

With some of Katrina's unidentifiable sounds, my brain found it difficult to interpret or categorize them. There was one peculiar sound that was loud, deep, and echoing that was followed by strange vibrations and a sensation that seemed to come from the ground under my feet. I would soon discover that they were the sounds of massive tree roots lifting from the saturated ground as fifty to eighty-foot tall pines and great big oaks fell.

My mother and I began to pray, reciting the rosary. The children seemed to be comforted by the sound of our voices raised in prayer, and they settled down on a mattress on the floor. It was difficult to concentrate on the prayerful words, and my mind wandered off at times, just simply begging God for His protection. I pondered our decision not to evacuate. Katrina's noises would not stop; they went on for hours. It was as if they were the sounds of Satan's fury with a century of time allotted to torment.

We heard what sounded like fingernails slowly scraping a chalkboard, coming from a closed-off bedroom in the house. It was the huge oak tree at the rear of our house dragging its long branches along the roof and window panes. The roots of the large old oak were being pulled up by the ferocious winds. The realization that I could not predict which way the tree would fall gave way to frightening possibilities. Petrified, I shouted the obvious, "The tree might fall on the house!" My thoughts illogically spiraled. I started to move the furniture out of the bedroom as if that was a priority. "Help me move everything out," I pleaded. Mike gave me a quizzical look and then yelled over the howling wind, "Get out of the room, now!" He was right. My panic brought me to a new level of helplessness and vulnerability. I had no choice but to surrender in prayer: "Please God, place your angels around that tree and hold it up." That once beautiful and admired tree had now become our enemy.

Hours after a long period of nonstop worrying, the winds finally died down. The strange sounds and vibrations stopped. Miraculously, no tree fell on the house. The hurricane passed. We were grateful to be alive.

"Thank you, God," my heart sighed. Feeling confident that the worst was over, we ventured outside. At the outset, the damage seemed minor, especially given the fact that we had survived. Debris was everywhere, in every direction we turned. Trees were down on our property: twenty-six tall pines and six gigantic oaks. Utility poles were either leaning or down, exposing wires as they lay about the dampness. Some were even submerged or floating in water. That cursed oak that worried me so took on a strange appearance, as if a spiritual battle had taken place between angels and demons: the branches slumped lifelessly, and although the trunk was upright, it looked as if something had clawed it to its death.

While surveying the storm's damage, I noticed the absence of noise. It was so strange. There were no dogs barking, no birds chirping, no sounds of cars or planes, no wind, no insects, not even the sound of people in the near distance. The only thing we heard was ourselves, our voices in the great big world. Life was abnormally still. There was a strange, intense heat, almost suffocating. The lack of oxygen resulted in a shortness of breath, making it difficult to expand our lungs. There was no breeze and no escape from the heat, not even in the shade. Between the lack of air to breathe and the debris strewn everywhere, we felt like we were the last people on earth—or in hell.

As we explored further, it became apparent that there was no way for a vehicle to pass through the streets and that our neighboring areas were in the same state for miles in every direction. Crossing our minds was the realization that no one could leave, and no one could come. Since communication was impossible due to damaged phone lines and cell towers, we wondered how long would we have to live without electricity, running water, news, and food. Different scenarios hit each person as the discovery of our isolation and limited conveniences was realized, revealing new personality temperaments of every person present. Everyone was roller coastering through mood swings, bringing out the worst and the best in people.

Hours later, our battery-operated radio picked up a single station. We would huddle around it for hours, hoping to hear any helpful information. Initially, its format consisted of distant callers describing their eye-witness accounts, but then the radio announcer's voice took on an alarmed tone. He began to report more emerging catastrophic news. The water pressure breached the saturated levees that protected the city of New Orleans and its suburban towns, causing urgent, life-threatening calamities. Water levels from a few feet to those causing complete submersion of homes were being reported. People thought they had survived the worst, but suddenly they were fighting for their lives: the water rose quickly, within minutes, and for some, it all happened in just seconds. With the fast-rising water, people had to move very quickly, and in only one direction: up. Many climbed to their attics or rooftops while fighting incoming and infested waters. Naturally, my heart sank at the thought of people drowning and at the thought of those who were physically incapable of reaching higher ground: the elderly, the bedridden, those with special needs, and the parents with more children than their arms could carry to safety. I thought about our family members who lived in those flooding cities, wondering where they were. Did they evacuate or escape? Were they trapped in their attics?

As we listened to more reports on the radio and awaited more details, bone-chilling cell calls came in from people who were literally fighting for their lives in the rising water. I will never forget one caller, a woman in distress, crying. Through the static, I clearly heard her despairing, quivering voice: "I have water in my house. I have water in my house. I'm going to drown. I can't swim. Water is everywhere. It is up to my waist. Everywhere in the house."

"Can you get out?" the radio announcer asked.

"No, it's rising so quickly. I don't know what to do." In a state of shock, she kept repeating herself over and over.

"Get up on your roof, now!" he told her.

"I can't—I have to hold my baby; she is only two months old."

The announcer projected a concerned voice, instructing, "Take the baby and get up on your roof, now!"

Crying and in hysterics, she yelled, "I have no food for my baby, no formula, my baby is hungry. I can't swim."

The call was lost . . . Tears streamed down my face as I felt a weight of sadness. I still cry writing this today.

Those who survived the flooding by escaping to a scorching roof or attic had no food or water. They kept company with the surrounding bacteria-infested black waters inhabited by rodents and snakes.

Many waited rescue with no relief from the intense, scorching heat, baking for hours. Some waited for days. Swimming to safety often resulted in being cut up by debris that was hidden below the dark waters. Despite the fact that some areas had strong drifts, some people chose to risk it and search for neighbors.

Even within our own neighborhood, we knew people needed help. There was an elderly man across the street, an eccentric, angry recluse. He did not live in his house, but in the garage, which was converted into a small apartment. In my seven years of living in the neighborhood, I had seen this man only three times. Neighbors shared horror stories about his wild parties and penchant for pornographic decor. Was this true or just rumor? The first time I laid eyes on him, he was urinating in his front yard. I gave him the benefit of the doubt, thinking, "Well, we do live in the country!"

We needed to check on him to make sure he was alive. Knowing his reputation for making enemies made the task undesirable. Somehow, I found myself heading over to his garage with food. I struggled to pull open the squeaky, weather-worn screen door that dragged, scraping the concrete. First I knocked on his door lightly, hoping he wouldn't answer, that maybe he had evacuated. Realizing my foolishness, I asked myself, "How could he leave, Anne? He doesn't even have a car, and no one can get out or into the neighborhood anyway." I knocked harder and called out his name, but still no answer. I entertained the thought of going home, but I knew it wouldn't be right. In an effort to repair my heart's intentions before leaving, I knocked a third time, even harder, and turned the doorknob. It was unlocked. I pushed the door open just a little and called his name. Finally, he answered me. There he stood. His peculiar appearance stunned me. I could feel my blood pressure begin to elevate. The mystery man of the neighborhood and I were face to face. His hair was wild, gray, and down to his shoulders. His clothes were filthy. His fingernails were yellow, long and dirty. He had psoriasis from his knees down, which appeared to be infected, and his shorts were stained with urine. I offered him food. He accepted it with a dry "thank you."

I asked, "Do you need anything? Do you have water?"

"No, I want a Diet Coke," he replied.

Twice a day I checked on him, bringing him food and water. The visits became a part of my daily post-Katrina routine. He would never come outside, except during the morning when the sun just began to rise. From across the street, I'd catch a glimpse of him in the distance, sitting in a chair just a few feet from his screened door, the door that led into the big world, our neighborhood. He retreated just like Mrs. Bordelon across the street did when I was a kid. Concerned, I wondered how he survived each day in that closed off, hot, humid garage apartment. Because his reputation preceded him, my children were afraid to bring him food. However, they agreed to walk with me halfway and watch for my return. Having heard some of the stories about him, I kept my guard up. "If I don't return in five minutes," I'd tell the kids, "go get your dad for help."

One day, instead of asking me for a Diet Coke, he asked, "Why are you doing this? Why are you being so nice to me?"

Only in my heart, I answered him in truth. "Because I fear God more than you."

He tried to pay me for the food. My refusal made him angry. As he hollered, a fountain of spit began to fly out of his mouth with each pronounced syllable. The louder he raised his voice, the further the spit flew. I watched, almost as if in slow motion, spit take flight from his mouth into mine. Immediately recalling what I had heard about his promiscuous lifestyle, I panicked, fearing a transmittable disease. My immediate instinct was to spit it out. Fearing an angry response from him, I refrained. Declining to swallow, I snatched the check he offered and sprinted home.

My youngest child, waiting at the halfway point, realized something had happened. "What's wrong, mama?"

Desperately trying to hold my mouth wide open, I felt saliva dripping down my chin. Without closing my mouth, I answered, "Get out of my way. He spit in my mouth."

I ran to the bathroom sink and started spitting like a prize-fighter. Grabbing the Listerine, I gargled, rinsing out my mouth over and over again. My sons walked into the house, and my youngest child yelled what seemed to be the big news of the day: "He spit in mom's mouth, and she's afraid she's going to get a disease!"

I replied very seriously to the boys, "Don't tell your father; he will never kiss me again."

The kids laughed hysterically.

My reclusive neighbor always took the food that was offered to him, but the way he accepted it was different every time. Perhaps he too was dealing with his own post-Katrina stress. He wanted to dictate to me how to prepare his food and when deliveries were to be made, otherwise he would not open his door. He would let me know if the food I brought him was to his liking or not. Sometimes, frustrated, I replied, "It's peanut butter and jelly, just like everyone else and that's all I got."

His morning chair was placed right in front of the door, which always made it awkward to get around. When Mike would accompany me on deliveries to our misanthropic friend, Mike would move his chair in an effort to clear the doorway. Upon leaving, I would move the chair back exactly as it was. I knew its placement was his quick recovery back into his safe environment. I don't think he really grasped the impact Katrina had made on people or the region. His world was his garage.

Our communication with each other was limited and sometimes strained, but in our relationship, a mutual understanding of trust had been achieved. As the days passed, I grew to care for someone most would consider an unlovable neighbor.

For every Katrina survivor, the inconvenience of having no electricity, along with the humid weather made every day seem to blend into the next. The survivors adopted a persevering attitude. With a spirit of determination, they initiated the restructuring of their lives and businesses, knowing neither would be the same ever again.

CHAPTER 12

Snowballs in My New Orleans

Live Today for Tomorrow

A post-Katrina house

K atrina cut a 415-mile-wide swath, and her winds of more than 100 miles per hour created twenty-two to twenty-eight-foot tidal surges. As numerous waterways overtopped and levees breached, many greater New Orleans area cities flooded, bringing eight to twelve feet of water inside homes and businesses. Cars were picked up by the rushing water, and houses lifted from their foundations and floated away. Even the Mississippi Gulf Coast experienced extensive damage. Mississippi would feel Katrina's effects as far north as Hattiesburg. Katrina's path of "change" would not only alter people's land and homes, but would also change their lives.

Within hours of Katrina's passing, the atmosphere of uncertainty quickly resided. Most businesses in the affected areas remained closed for the next few days, weeks, and months, and some closed forever. Although most people could not report to work, what manifested was the natural human inclination to be physically productive. Neighbors helped neighbors remove trees off homes and place tarps over open roof holes. Within our own compound, energetic work efforts began with everyone participating in chores, clearing away the debris that surrounded the property, and dragging tree limbs into big piles. Washing clothes required scrubbing laundry by hand. I soon realized the importance and necessity of a washboard, the kind that was used back in the day. Another chore was to serve as an impromptu chef at the barbecue pit, creating healthy meals using the limited food supply in the pantry. Styling in the "do-rag" tied around my head, I'd call out the day's "special" menu: "Tuna-cake surprise with canned green beans heating up on the grill." While performing these tasks, it was easy for me to escape and daydream. I thought about being in the air conditioned jewelry store, wishing I was making jewelry for people celebrating one of life's happy events. As my thoughts shifted towards our customers, I became concerned for them and hoped that they had weathered Katrina safely. Soon my mind turned toward questioning my ancestors: why would they want to migrate to New Orleans, a city that is humidly hot and prone to hurricanes? As I reflected, I began to realize why.

I am a second-generation American on my father's side of the family. My grandfather, who was an immigrant from Sicily, came to America at the age of sixteen, courageously carrying his dreams and a desire to live a better life, one filled with opportunity. I was told that as he settled into his new home, New Orleans, he discovered that much like his homeland, it too was rich in both community and culture. The land for farming was also similar to that of the Old Country. Many Sicilians immigrated to New Orleans, and at one time, New Orleans had more Italians than New York City. New Orleans also possessed the bustle of a big city with a quaint, small town feel. This is why he made New Orleans his home.

Because he spoke very little English, it was easier for him to adopt a self-reliant means of employment, one that was familiar to him. Since he grew up on a farm, he had a working knowledge about the production of produce and the meat-to-market process. Ambitious in his entrepreneurial spirit, he would eventually operate his own market.

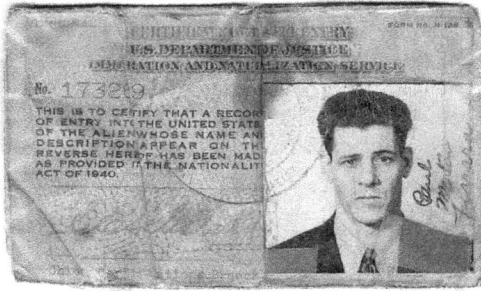

Anne's Grandfather, Paul Saverio Martin Ferrara

Most of Louisiana's immigrants, including Italians, arrived here through the Port of New Orleans. As the city swelled, families began building beyond the city's borders. Neighborhoods expanded into the newly-established parishes surrounding the city, creating what became known as Greater New Orleans. And although they moved, their hearts did not. They brought with them their appreciation for a certain way of life, a certain way of thinking, their traditions, and a unique harmonized blend of personality traits. These were friendly, compassionate, life-loving people, confident in who they were and filled with an appreciation for where they came from. Even today, most Louisiana children are raised with the same blend of cultural qualities that are dear to their ancestors' hearts.

I thought about how the New Orleanians, no matter what generation, are not only proud, but protective of their heritage. At times we are saddened by the commercialization within the city, especially those changes that have no connection to our families' pasts. Most visitors do not realize that we are not entertained or defined by the confused, poor souls who display demoralizing behavior on Bourbon Street; they bring down the beauty of our city. We don't even care for the discussions about how one thinks he or she can get free beads during Mardi Gras; that's for the shallow rookie visitor who really doesn't know New Orleans. However, we welcome all guests, including out-of-state newcomers who think they have arrived to "fix" or "improve" us, whether it's in public affairs or local television and radio. We give them a pass.

Our ingrained, unique culture can be found throughout the state. Louisianians are in love with family, food, and good times. We enjoy telling or hearing a good story, not only during a gathering, but while helping a neighbor. Friendly greetings are quickly offered to guests—we will strike up a conversation with anyone. The French word "lagniappe" sums up the character of the people: we give a little something extra because our hearts are celebratory, overflowing with a flair for life.

Within the drifting thoughts, I began to entertain the creative side of my brain, designing jewelry that would capture the heart of New Orleanians and the beautiful spirit displayed by the first responders in Katrina's aftermath. Creative designs whirled around in my head, and at the same time, I delighted in reliving some of my New Orleans memories.

One memory that especially stood out in my mind was that of Mardi Gras when I was a child. At 5:00 am in the morning, mama would wake me and my sisters up; it was Mardi Gras Day. Quickly, we jumped out of bed and put on our homemade costumes. One year, I was a cowgirl. Another year, I was a hippy. Each year, the costume was a character relative to my age. I remember mama insisting that we eat before leaving for the parades, but we were so excited about our day that we didn't want to have breakfast.

Daddy, joining in on the excitement, hurried us to beat the morning traffic, and into the car we piled. Back then, no one wore seat belts and in order for us all to fit, we sat snug together. Somehow, I always maneuvered to sit by a window. My mission was to see other people driving by in their costumes too. Sometimes, I saw masked people up on a float speeding by, as if on a flying carpet. Its decorative fringe quickly whizzed by as they raced into the city for the parade lineup. With my head sticking out the open window, I waved, yelling, "Throw me something, mister!" Our drive to the biggest party in the world seemed way too long, even though it was just twenty minutes.

Anticipating the day's events, my imagination was filled with wonder, thoughts of seeing incredible, colorful costumes, of hearing rhythmic, drumming music, and of catching throws that were magical treasures. Prepared, I had my big bag in hand, ready for the challenge of catching the most unusual and cherished throws. One special catch is the hand-painted coconut from the Zulu parade. Every year, I asked my dad to help me catch a golden coconut. A few times we got lucky, but when we weren't, I happily settled for pretty, colorful beads, a water gun, or even a big, plastic fake cigar.

Because of the thick crowds, my dad parked on the outskirts of the parade routes. He and my mom tightly held our wrists, pulling us through the lively crowds in the Vieux Carré, as my eyes helplessly wandered. We would go past the Krystal hamburger place—mmm, they smelled so good! Then past Russell Stover, the chocolate store— yum! Then down to the big parade stands which were in front of a ritzy hotel. Fortunately, my dad was a well-known musician in New Orleans and was invited to view the parades from the stands. This was such a privilege for us meager street kids because we believed that the stands were where the rich people sat for Mardi Gras. As we entered the fancy hotel, my sisters and I marveled at all the shiny, bright crystal decorations. Riding up in the elevator, we waited for our tummies to tingle. Smiling at our impressed little faces was the man who worked the elevator. "Hello. Going up?" he would ask in a deep voice.

Watching the numbers light up above the elevator doors just added to our excitement. The doors opened to a huge, grand room.

Mama said it was a ballroom where people dressed up lavishly and danced like Cinderella. My shoes tapped on the floor as I walked across the big room. Passing by the room's open wrought-iron balconies, I was offered an enchanting view of the streets in the French Quarter. Close by, a doorway led to the parade stands, which were filled with party goers, some in costumes. I spent the rest of my day sandwiched between many big people, catching the best throws. Sometimes, this was to my advantage. Either I was blocked from the stinging, glass bead necklaces thrown from the floats, or the adults handed me, the little kid, their throws. In the stands, my sisters and I were eye level with the people on the floats, but this time the floats were not racing by. If eye contact was achieved with someone on a float, you were almost guaranteed a throw.

At the end of the day, my bag was overflowing with throws, almost too heavy to carry. Walking back to the car to head home, I was always exhausted, my arms tired from holding them high in the air. But I hugged my bag of throws like a precious treasure as I tried to see over it. These colorful childhood memories instilled in me a feeling that anything was possible, no matter who you were.

Smiling ear to ear as I thought about Mardi Gras as a child, I was snapped back to Katrina's reality by a family member who was asking what could I possibly be grinning about. I returned to my Katrina duties again, dragging jagged, weighty tree limbs.

Doing outdoor chores in the heat made time pass slowly. Trying to catch my breath, I searched for just a small, merciful breeze. Taking rest under a big oak tree on my property, I eagerly escaped to reflect again.

As a little girl, my father would take my sisters and me to the City Park in New Orleans. A familiar sight was the park's beautiful, century-old, huge oak trees draped in Spanish moss. Our favorite pastime at the park was to swing on the huge constructed welded metal swings that seemed to stand twenty feet high in the air. As we would swing, we stretched, trying to touch the clouds with our toes, or we imagined that we were flying above the trees. Afterward, dad would take us over to the park's famous fountain to wade in with a bunch of other kids hoping to cool down from the summer heat. On the drive home, he would take us for a special treat, a snowball. "Any flavor you want!" he exclaimed. Spearmint was my favorite. After just about four bites, our lips and teeth turned the color of our snowball. Showing off our bright, new smiles, we laughed at each other.

With a quick slap on my arm to squash a blood-thirsty mosquito that was drawn to my sweat, I snapped back to the duties of the storm's aftermath. How I would appreciate a snowball in that moment. It was time to cook over the hot pit and feed the family, however.

Still, with New Orleans heavy on my mind, and with the heat from the grill rising up from cooking something lame like canned vegetables, it was easy to torment myself with thoughts of tasty, wonderfully-flavored New Orleans food: a cup of gumbo, boiled seafood, or a fresh, crispy fried shrimp po-boy with the right amount of hot sauce, just like when we went out to the West End restaurants on Lake Pontchartrain. My favorite place there was a seafood restaurant built on a pier that sat over the lake. It kept its numerous windows open in the summer evenings so you could feel the lake's breeze. While we waited for our fried shrimp po-boys, we watched and listened to the small, tranquil waves and sipped on an icy, New Orleans Barq's root beer.

Even with all the uncertainty of Katrina's aftermath, we still found ways to have good times with the family. One evening after a lackluster, but appreciated dinner, we gathered around the battery-operated radio for some news. With no music to be heard, my dad began to drum on the table and whistle the tune "Do You Know What It Means to Miss New Orleans?" For the next few glorious minutes, we were all transported far away from our concerns to "the city that care forgot." In our minds, we were surrounded by the sights and sounds of the heart of the city. The music had even more "soul" because my dad, the real deal, an authentic New Orleans Jazz drumming musician, played and sang for us. He possessed a natural and creative rhythm that he was born with, a talent that came from within his New Orleanian soul.

Moved with emotional thoughts and sentiments, I sat down by candlelight and sketched the design that would become known as a badge of honor for New Orleans. The jewelry design "I Know What It Means to Love New Orleans®" was created that night.

I Know What It Means to Love New Orleans®

Feeling inspired, I wrote:

My New Orleans

You can find New Orleans on a map bordered by the 17th Street Canal, Lake Pontchartrain, the mighty Mississippi River, and the Gulf of Mexico.

You will also find New Orleans in the hearts of the Louisiana people and those around the world who have experienced it . . . Jazz, Mardi Gras, The French Quarter, Creole, and Cajun Cuisine.

But my New Orleans is more. It is bigger. The Big Easy goes beyond the borderlines of this great city. It is always a part of me, wherever I go.

*My New Orleans goes north, up the Mississippi River
to Natchez, strung together by mighty oak trees, Spanish
moss, and a path of majestic plantation homes from an
era gone by.*

*My New Orleans goes east where my family vacationed
on the sandy, white beaches of Waveland, Gulfport, and
Biloxi.*

*My New Orleans goes south through the bayous and
swamps, where, as a young girl, my father took me fishing
down the Mississippi Delta and to the Gulf of Mexico.*

*My New Orleans gets its spice from the west, through
Baton Rouge and to the heart of Acadia (Cajuns) to
Lafayette.*

*My New Orleans is like a good gumbo with all the
necessary ingredients to make a recipe rich in culture.
A gumbo that is stirred by a people whose southern
hospitality welcomes each ingredient to melt into the
other, to give it the flavor of something you will always
take with you wherever you go. Once you taste it . . . you
will know what it means to love New Orleans.*

That's my home . . . that's my New Orleans.

During the aftermath of Katrina, we were without conveniences and transported to a simpler time: nothing cold to drink
in the heat, no snacking between meals, and grateful for any food
that was on the dinner plate. Labor-intensive chores we cursed,
but the reward of rest was physically gratifying. We had to excuse
each other's bodily odors from perspiration, but soon were relieved
that our bodies began to change as they adapted to the heat. Cold
showers became refreshing. Our body temps adjusted, cooling
down at night, sometimes allowing us to sleep covered with light

blankets. We looked forward to visiting with each other, especially during the evening at dinner. We spent quality time together. We had no TV, no computers, no cell phones, no distractions, and we weren't in a hurry.

Anne hanging laundry while Michael hauls tree branches, Post-Katrina

The hardest part of Katrina was the unknown: what would tomorrow bring? We had to live each day before we could live for tomorrow. But we became closer as a family, depending on each other and, more importantly, on God.

CHAPTER 13

Dan Aykroyd

To Give is To Receive

Dan Aykroyd posing with badge

Without electricity during the post-Katrina weeks, curfews were mandated, the sale of liquor was prohibited, and precautionary neighborhood checkpoints were established. The nightly abyss of Katrina's darkness required law and order to protect potential victims and guard vacant property. Even at home, we kept our guns loaded and our generator chained to our tractor at all times. Law Enforcement from other states, such as the New York Police Department, came to assist.

Post-Katrina weeks seemed long, but with each passing day life did get a little easier. Gradually, electricity was being restored, but only within areas with less damage. Unfortunately, our rural neighborhood needed more allotted cleaning efforts and repair, and we were told it could take months before we would have electricity. But to our good fortune, the electricity to the jewelry store was restored, and so we naturally gravitated to it. While we soaked up the much-appreciated chill of the air conditioning, we cleaned up our water and mold-damaged jewelry store. Mike and I, concerned for the future of our business, pondered who would buy jewelry during a time like this. Figuring we had plenty of time on our hands, we began to work on creating the badge of honor, titled "I Know What It Means to Love New Orleans®," dedicating our efforts to first responders.

The first prototype badges were cast in sterling silver and packaged with the write-up. They were ready to be presented to those who took on leadership roles. As I mapped out a distribution route around the greater New Orleans cities, I tried to keep in mind the mandated restrictions on the purchase of gasoline. Gas was rationed for government and utility vehicles, along with certain necessary businesses that were operating on generators. At home, we too were running on a generator and understood the value of gasoline. We only ran it during certain times of the day.

One of those leaders was the police chief of Harahan, Peter Dale, who welcomed and organized the efforts of the New York Police Department. Chief Dale seemed inundated with phone calls and the task of delegating duties to his deputies. However, he took a few minutes to graciously accept the badge. As quickly as we greeted him, we had to leave him, hoping he would find time to read the write up. To my surprise, the next day he called me at the jewelry store.

"Anne, I have someone in my office that I showed the badge to."

I was grateful that he did take further notice of the badge.

"If I give him my badge, can you give me another?"

I had only casted a few. I thought for a moment and asked, "Who is it that you want to give it to?"

"Well . . . ," there was a pause, "Dan Aykroyd."

Doubting his response, I pressed.

"Dan Aykroyd? Dan Aykroyd is with you right now in your office? *The Blues Brothers, Ghostbusters*, Dan Aykroyd?"

"Yes," he stated simply.

Delighted that he thought enough of the badge to give it to him, I cried out, "Yes, yes, please give it to him! I will give you another."

My mind flooded with questions. I had to ask, "What is he doing in your office?"

Chief Dale replied, "He came down to help. He brought supplies. I'll tell you about it another time."

Before I could finish sharing with Mike what had just happened, the phone rang again. I answered, "Anne Dale Jeweller."

"Chief Dale here. Dan wants to buy five hundred of them." The chief lowered his voice, asking in a whisper, "Anne, can you make that many?"

Answering, I said, "Absolutely, only under one condition: I get to personally hand-deliver them to Dan Aykroyd myself."

Appreciating the opportunity, I asked if I could meet with him now and work out a few details. He agreed. As I hung up the phone, it occurred to me that my disheveled appearance was a reminder of my electricity-free conditions, which meant an unkempt hair-do and no ironed clothes. I wasn't looking my best to meet such a celebrity. The small amount of gas in the car also worried me. I knew that a thirty mile-plus road trip could leave me stranded somewhere. Mike, being supportive of the idea, knew I wanted the opportunity and encouraged me to go. I jumped in my car, hoping that I would find a gas station at some point. I headed south toward the city of Harahan to meet Mr. Aykroyd. To conserve on gas, I decided not to run the air conditioner until I was within a mile of our meeting, so as to not look or smell too sweaty.

I had never met a movie star, so I didn't know what to expect. Before getting out of the van, I took one last quick look in the mirror, as many women do, and then stopped dead in my tracks. It was the first time in over three weeks I took a hard look at myself. I noticed Katrina's effect on my face. My skin was that of an older woman from the heat, and the stress deeply imbedded the number eleven into my forehead from worry. My wire-gray hairs were in need of coloring and smoothing. Observing my hands, I saw that my nails were broken, and I had calloused palms from cleaning. My pride and vanity had slapped me in the face with a dose of reality as to the true meaning of beauty and the important things in life. Meeting Mr. Aykroyd was a test for me to see if I could let go of my pride and keep focused on what I was trying to accomplish. I wiped away the mascara and eyeliner that had melted under my worn black eyes and prayed, "God, thank you for this opportunity and for my creative talents. Thank you for sparing my family from serious injury and great loss from Katrina. Please bless me with this visit and help me to accomplish all that I need for the success of this badge. Please allow me to be the voice of those in need."

Feeling somewhat rejuvenated by the fact I was on a mission, I drew my energy from the badge. As I walked toward our agreed meeting location, I initially did not notice that Mr. Aykroyd was standing in front of a door, politely waiting for me. I almost said, "Excuse me," and walked right past him, but when I heard him say, "Oh, here she is," I knew it was him. He said it with a huge, inviting smile, and he was bursting with energy, as if he was ready to roll up his sleeves and go to work. Despite his Hollywood status, he seemed at ease, as if Louisiana was a familiar home to him. Because Katrina brought about anxiety and much sadness, his happiness was something my heart had not seen in people in several weeks; it was a refreshing emotion that was truly missed.

Awkwardly, I apologized for not immediately recognizing him, then I quickly introduced myself. He was engaging and sincere. He genuinely liked the concept of the badge and understood what I was trying to accomplish without having to explain much. At the end of our conversation, I clumsily began to ask him for a photograph when he kindly interrupted me and suggested, "Why don't we take a picture together with me holding the badge?" He was one step ahead of me the whole time. After posing with the badge, he politely asked if the badge was his to keep. I said, "Of course."

After meeting with Mr. Aykroyd, I walked away awestruck at how things were favorably unfolding before my eyes. Inspired with hope, I thanked God for the blessed opportunity and prayed for the wisdom and strength to forge ahead.

Back home, it took almost thirty days for our electricity to be restored. My priorities in life were different because I had changed. Getting back to some familiar pre-Katrina routines, I pulled out my finest china for everyday use: What was I saving it for? I appreciated even the smallest things, like walking into a room and turning on a light with the flip of a switch. I also knew it was time for a strange farewell delivery to my reclusive neighbor. I brought over a plate of home-cooked food and, as he reached for the plate with one hand, he tightly grabbed hold of my other wrist. I was startled, but I didn't feel threatened. I didn't know what to think or to say. I just froze and stared at him. I saw a connection in his eyes, along with some tears. He said, "You have no idea what you have done for me."

In that unforgotten moment, I saw Christ. It was as if Jesus was speaking. Moved with humility, I too teared up. In my heart, I felt an overwhelming sense of gratitude that I was given the opportunity to feed him, to serve him. Never would I have dreamed that I would feel sad that my mission of serving my neighbor would come to an end. I also felt sorrowful that I had never done anything for my neighbor in the past seven years. As he let go of my wrist, slowly the words that escaped my mouth were, "You . . . are . . . welcome." It seemed that my reply, or any reply could never measure up to the sincerity expressed by him. Astonished by what had just happened and at a loss for words, I asked him if he needed anything else. "No," he insisted as he turned to take the plate inside. "A friend who is returning from evacuating is coming to help me," he said.

Awkwardly, we said goodbye. At home while sitting in a chair in silence and reflecting on what had just happened, I realized that every moment, from the smells to the spit, was worth it. I wondered if he felt Christ in that heavenly moment too. I vowed from that day forward to continue checking on him.

A few days later, I had to take a business trip to London. Upon my return, I went to check on him, but halfway out the door my home phone rang. I went back to answer it. While I was on the phone, I heard a knock. I excused myself from the call and answered the door. There in the doorway stood a police officer. He didn't have to say anything. I knew. I was the first to speak.

"My neighbor is dead."

The officer replied, "Yes, he is."

It just was not meant for me to discover him dead.

With the news of his death, I felt a loss. I can only speculate that the heat and stress of Katrina took its toll on him. Seeking closure with the man who gave me one of the most profound "thank yous" in my life, I went to his converted garage apartment, as I had done many times before, but the door was locked. In search of something, anything, I went to his house, the house he once lived in, but that door was locked too. I really didn't know what I was looking for, perhaps remnants of something that told me more of who he was. I went home, still wondering. In my nightly reflections, I examined my need to get inside his house: was it because I felt responsible for him and wasn't there when he needed me? Was it because I didn't want to say goodbye to our profound moment? Or was it all just such an epic event, I didn't want it buried? To my surprise, as if a prayer had been answered, the next morning while sipping my coffee and looking through my kitchen window, I saw the front door of the old house ajar, as if it was an invitation to say goodbye. Putting my coffee down, I headed over. Pushing the door open further, I called out, "Hello," but no one answered. Then the thought occurred to me that someone may have broken in, and against my better judgment, I went in to explore. The house was messy: old dishes were piled in the sink with fossilized food, parts of the roof were missing, and large spider webs were about. I felt as if I were in the story of Great Expectations by Charles Dickens. I looked around at a few photographs he had hung on the walls, but they really didn't tell me much. His life was in that garage, and it was not for me to discover. As I walked out, the door closing behind me, I saw an old newspaper on the porch and jumping off the page was the word "reciprocity." Suddenly, I realized that what I was looking for wasn't in any house; it was something within me. Complete closure was not to be. He made me a better person, and it was in giving that I received.

The first responders were some of Katrina's best people demonstrating reciprocity, and Mr. Aykroyd wanted to reward their kind actions. After making five hundred badges for his special order, I had the privilege of being invited to his celebratory event where he distributed the badges, honoring and personally thanking hundreds of first responders at the House of Blues in New Orleans. The honored law enforcement represented many different roles and ranks, but they all seemed to have similarities in their psychological makeup. They may have appeared different, but they talked the same talk, they walked the same walk. In short, they answered the same call—to serve and protect. The tragedies and triumphs experienced during and after Katrina bonded them as they shared a camaraderie. For them, this event was a commemorative moment that acknowledged their calling, their work, and their impact on the lives of people.

In his basic black suit, Mr. Aykroyd's face beamed, and the buzz in the room only amplified his energy. People were happy, and that made him happy. I watched him as he took picture after picture with anyone who wanted one; he posed for hundreds, if not thousands of photos. Cameras flashed continuously, strobing for more than an hour. The bright, pulsating lights would have caused anyone who was sensitive to have a seizure. Even as a spectator, I had to look away many times. But through all of this, Mr. Aykroyd continued to smile and was humbly patient. Curious, I watched him from a distance, like I used to watch the blind man when I was younger. I studied his character and how he handled people. For Mr. Aykroyd, it was a never-ending pull of people tugging at him. Every so often, he broke away, rubbing his eyes from the flashes and shaking his head a bit. Then he pulled a genuine gracious spirit from a special place within and again offered it to anyone who asked. In his efforts, he never tired of moving around the room, greeting people, talking with them, shaking hands, smiling and laughing. I was so impressed by his graciousness towards Katrina's best.

But Mr. Aykroyd's concern for Louisiana's rebuilding efforts did not end there. I asked if I could set up an interview with him for a radio talk show I hosted. Generously, he responded yes. He explained his schedule was usually full when he visits New Orleans, but he would manage to give me a call. Eight months after Katrina, one Sunday afternoon, my cell phone rang.

"Anne, this is Dan."

I was surprised and impressed that he remembered. He scheduled the interview, settling on a place and time. That very night, around midnight, we were to meet in front of the House of Blues. When I hung up the phone, I thought to myself, "Midnight? I hope I can stay awake."

Knowing that people were still struggling in the aftermath of Katrina, my hope was that the interview would lift the spirits of hurricane victims. Some people still had no home or no job to return to. Those with absolutely nothing but a cement slab found that others were more fortunate. Some people at least had some personal artifacts to salvage as they rummaged through the Katrina slush. For them, it could be a find that recalled a happy memory, even if it was a moldy framed picture, a corroded piece of jewelry, or a blackened kitchen tool. Such discoveries sometimes sent the victim deeper into depression. And sometimes the found object could bring about a new realization—a jolt of reality that the only true treasures are really in the heart.

Ongoing tension rose between homeowners and their Katrina guests, causing horrific family feuds and conflicts too painful for many family members to even discuss today. Insurance companies were playing games with people's lives as they delayed or refused payments. Supply and demand caused dramatic spikes in the cost of new homes and reconstruction, making repairs or rebuilding difficult. It was more than some people could handle, and the effects were terrible: the stress broke marriages, mental institutions were at full capacity, and the suicide rate skyrocketed. Katrina's disruption literally killed people. Page after page, I read the names and stories that filled the obituary section of the newspaper.

Witnessing these hardships motivated me to do more, and I looked forward to the interview with one of the world's most beloved comedic actors during a very heavy-hearted period for Louisiana.

Midnight was around the corner, and Mike patiently waited with me outside the House of Blues. While waiting, we sat on the street curb, people-watching. As I watched for Mr. Aykroyd, I looked down both ends of the street. Appearing in the shadows of the famous New Orleans street lights were tourists humming tunes and couples embracing in the "Big Easy." We even spotted legendary musician Doctor John strolling down the street, chatting with likeminded people about music. Being absorbed in the voices and music of the French Quarter reminded me that it was the first time I had visited the city since Katrina. It all rekindled my love for the city. Midnight came and went. Every passing minute brought on concern that Mr. Aykroyd may have changed his plans. But before I knew it, true to his word, he arrived with a caravan of people, delightfully laughing from an appetite sated by New Orleans food and fare. Quickly, I stood, positioning myself so that he wouldn't walk past. Now it was my turn to wait in front of a door for him.

Relieved, I said, "Dan, you're here. Are you ready for the interview?"

"Yes, follow me," he said.

Parting from his guests, off we went into the Parish entrance of the House of Blues. Searching for a quiet place to conduct the interview, we walked down a dark hallway that was guarded by a security man who led us to an elevator and then up to what's called the "Foundation Room." News of his presence must have traveled fast. The elevator doors opened. Loud with anticipation, the anxious crowd in the Foundation Room was elated by the sight of Mr. Aykroyd. Once again, I had the unique chance to study him, but this time I walked closely behind a celebrity. I watched how people spun their heads around quickly just to get a glimpse of him. I watched how people tried to find ways to get close to him and how some tried to keep their cool as he walked through the corridor.

We then entered a private room that had colorful fabric walls and ancient artifacts of Tibetan décor. We sat at a small table where I placed my recorder down. Considering how late it was, it was extraordinary that again he had that familiar burst of energy. He was ready to get to work.

The following are some excerpts from my interview with Mr. Aykroyd:

Anne and Dan Aykroyd

ANNE DALE: Where were you when Katrina hit? Did you see the levees break?

DAN AYKROYD: At that time, I was in Los Angeles when we saw the devastation. We saw what had to be done. We loaded up my friend's tractor trailer with boats, rubbers, t-shirts, everything; even sanitary napkins. We drove into Louisiana about two weeks after the storm, straight to Harahan, then drove into New Orleans at night with Chief Dale and some of his armed men. At that time, there was no light or power at all. Water everywhere. We mainly went in to see if a friend of mine who lived in the Quarter was okay. No damage at all, but of course there was no one in the city but law enforcement, EMTs, first responders, rescue people. It was very interesting to see all the people who came from all over the world to help. It was fascinating and wonderful.

AD: You've done a great thing for New Orleans.

DA: Well, I love the city. I have been coming here every year since I was twenty-one. Here, we founded the House of Blues, which has been one of our strongest clubs, and it really fits great into the city. All our staff is local, and our management works with community to make sure that all these initiatives get known.

AD: They say that music heals the soul. Do you believe that?

DA: I definitely know it. I play frequently with my band, The Blues Brothers Formal Classic Revue. It does keep me young. It's the only hour and a half of my life where I don't have to think about business or obligations. I just get in that cradle of that music, and for an hour and half all I have to do is deliver those songs, deliver the dancing, and the harmonica. It makes me feel good. I really feel it's keeping me young.

AD: As a female jeweler, I have to ask: when you got engaged, how did you propose?

DA: Well, it was the worst time of the year. It was March in Canada, with mud streaming down into the roads and no leaves on the trees, and I brought her to, basically, a trailer, which was a shack, and said, "This is the worst time of my life. If you can deal with this, I wouldn't mind maybe putting a life together with you," and so she agreed that was something she would consider.

AD: Dan, thank you for all that you have done for the city.

DA: So many of the hardship stories turned out to demonstrate the resilience of the community here. And mostly, I never heard any complaints. I heard, "I lost my house, I lost this, but we'll be alright." Everybody said, "We'll be alright, I'll be alright, we'll get it back, we'll be back."

AD: That's what makes Louisiana people so great.

DA: Yeah, my favorite state. My favorite city.

AD: What do you want to be remembered for?

DA: Career-wise, there's not much I can do about being remembered because it's already out there, and I know I did some good things and some bad things, so people will remember me for whatever they liked in terms of the career. But I want to be remembered primarily as a father who passed on to my three daughters compassion and a love for humankind and an understanding for the equanimity of human beings—that we're all the same.

— § —

Mr. Aykroyd gave to Louisiana his presence and a fresh, caring face accompanied by a sincere heart during a difficult time. It was stirring for so many Louisianians that someone of his celebrity status genuinely cared. He "knows what it means to love New Orleans."

From the neighbor who taught me to be a better person to the famous celebrity who said "thank you" to the hundreds of first responders, I truly began to have a greater appreciation of what the badge represented—reciprocity.

Soon, the "I Know What It Means to Love New Orleans®" badges began to sell by the hundreds, then by the thousands. People gave the badge in recognition of others who had provided kind and thoughtful actions. Each day, people filled the store with surreal Katrina stories, and each person had their own hero, someone to thank.

CHAPTER 14
Katrina Heroes

Gratitude

Making of the "I Know What It Means to Love New Orleans®" badges

housands of badges have been sold. More than a piece of jewelry, the badge carries a message, a battle cry for healing and a desire to be reconnected and made whole again. Seeing the badge became an open invitation for onlookers to ask those wearing it to share Katrina stories, prompting an exchange of human compassion. As people flocked into the store to buy the badge, countless stories of hardship and heroism were told. Different versions of difficult situations were shared, from those who were in the midst of the chaos in the Superdome to those hiding in hotel rooms in downtown New Orleans for days or weeks. People expressed relief and related stories of being rescued by boat from their second-floor homes and rooftops, stories of where they had fled to escape the flood waters. I heard accounts of deaths, suicides, saved lives, chain-saw accidents, charitable handouts being distributed, homemade barricades built by fearful neighborhoods, lost family members, and found family members. The things people experienced and witnessed would impact them forever. The jewelry store became a hub where people came to visit and talk, needing to tell their story of survival as they wept tears or burst into laughter, both of which were part of the recovery process. Unimaginable stories of Katrina's effects were told. . . .

— § —

Hiding from rampant crime and looters, an elderly white woman took refuge on the eighth floor of an empty hotel in New Orleans. Listening to her battery-powered radio, she was frightened by the national news reports speculating that most crimes had something to do with race. Alone inside of her hotel room at night, she heard sounds coming from the nearby vacant rooms. These sounds were sometimes accompanied by gunshots. Days later, she realized that without food and water, she had to leave or she would die in her sealed, abandoned hotel room. Physically weak, she began to make her way out. She encountered an African American man with his family. He carried her weak, frail body several city blocks above the flooded waters to a dry, safe area, keeping her from harm's way. Racism was not prevalent as the media had portrayed. She came to the store to buy her hero a badge.

— § —

A handful of women shared their terrifying stories of living in the Superdome. The number of evacuees in the Superdome far outnumbered National Guard personnel. National Guard troops were assaulted by some of Katrina's worst in the Dome and some soldiers feared for their lives too.

While the National Guard tried to get the chaos under control, rumors of women being raped in bathrooms and people being mugged in tucked-away corners kept them from leaving each other's side. The women witnessed food being distributed in the Dome, only to those who were strong and able to grab first. They watched adults and children get trampled. Crippled by fear and disgusted with overflowing toilets in deplorable conditions, the women told stories of soiling themselves. One of the ladies started her menstrual cycle and sought assistance from the National Guard. A male guard offered her bottled water and sanitary napkins to clean herself. Behind a lifted blanket, guarded by her friends, she did just that.

These women came to the jewelry store to buy badges as a symbol to never forget their courage and loyalty to each other during those dark times.

— § —

Disconcertingly, a national news media outlet reporting updates on the post-Katrina events helicoptered over a stranded couple who sat on their roof. The news crew snapped an infamous picture of them for the world to see but left the couple stranded for days without food or water. It was insensitive and inhumane. No rescue was provided, nor were supplies dropped to them. They waited two more days before being rescued. Grateful that they survived and had each other, they came to buy a badge for themselves.

— § —

A customer purchased a badge for a construction worker who was employed to demolish homes with a bulldozer in a Katrina-devastated neighborhood. In the midst of the demolition, the worker spotted something moving inside one of the homes. The movement was unlike that of scurrying animals. Uncertain as to what he saw, he turned off the bulldozer and went into the home where he discovered three children, alone in hiding. The children's missing parents were never found, not even their bodies. Heroism would continue—all three children would eventually be adopted together.

— § —

A customer wanted her aunt, who had a special-needs child, to evacuate with her, but the aunt insisted that specialized assistance was coming for them to accommodate her child's wheelchair. No one ever came. After Katrina, they were discovered in their home: they died as they embraced each other. The niece purchased a badge in their honor.

— § —

The badge has honored good Samaritans everywhere, from those who saw the Louisiana license plate of a family of refugees and offered them money to those who took in family members, acquaintances, and in some cases, to those who were complete strangers and became friends for life.

The badge also went beyond anything I initially envisioned. It evolved into a shared symbol of tragedies and triumphs, an emblem of human generosity. Each day, the staff worked very hard to see to it that the thousands of badges ordered from the store's website or by phone were delivered all around the U.S. and even to other countries. Some days, we filled sacks of internet orders. Due to the sacks' immense weight, we had to drive to the post office that was just across the street.

Local and national celebrities bought or received the badge. A customer who worked as an extra in a movie starring Brad Pitt in New Orleans said she gave him the badge on his birthday. She expressed that it was a gift to him for helping Katrina victims.

I would see the badge on many people, from musicians to noted chefs, from politicians to strangers walking by me on the street. I saw people on television wear it; even a senator wore it during a State of the Union Address delivered by President George W. Bush on national television. I received letters of thanks from the Louisiana governor, President Bush, and Pope Benedict XVI.

Katrina, a category five hurricane with winds up to 175 mph, left areas of New Orleans devastated and abandoned; some areas resembled bombed war zones. Breached levees flooded a 145-

square mile area, the size of Washington, D.C. Its damage was estimated at $89.6 billion. There were 1,836 confirmed deaths, and 705 people were reported as missing. No amount of planning could have prepared anyone for the destruction, turmoil, and disruption to daily life. Victims could not make sense of it, but they searched to find hope in the aftermath.

Katrina formed as many heroes as she did victims, and those adversely affected purchased badges for their champions as a symbol of their heartened expression of appreciation.

CHAPTER 15

Return to New Orleans

Help From the Divine

Archbishop Phillip Hannan holding the jewelry design featuring
Our Lady of Prompt Succor on the celebratory day, January 8th
at the National Shrine in New Orleans

L ouisianians have always overcome difficulties. The first settlers combated the inconveniences of swamps—not to mention surviving malaria, floods, and oil spills—and subsequent generations were forced to rebuild after wars and hurricanes. Such hardships affect not only individuals but also communities, and those past difficult times remind us of what is truly important in life—faith, family and community. We appreciate the things we are blessed with.

Louisianians also share a deep and abiding bond that suggests we are all related in some way. In a simple encounter between locals, this relationship is demonstrated by an introductory question,

"Where are your people from?" It is a respectful search for common ground, acknowledging each other's ancestral connection. People usually answer this question by naming their hometown, followed by the name of their mama and daddy's hometown. "Kenner, but mama and daddy are from New Orleans," as if everyone knows your parents, all being one and the same.

Louisianians live life outwardly as expressive people. We share with others life's triumphs and defeats and are happier for it. Passion just comes naturally for Louisianians, as it is inherited by each generation in the same way the contagious festive attitude of "Laissez Les Bons Temps Rouler" ("Let the Good Times Roll") is passed down to our children. Louisianians truly are one big family.

It is also said that Louisianians find any reason to have a party. This is true. When it comes to revelry, we have the ability to celebrate even the simplest things, making the most of any opportunity. Just about anything Louisiana harvests, creates, uses, or eats, we build a festival around: petroleum, music, wooden boats, Creole tomatoes, seafood, and reptiles just to mention a few. We bring an element of panache and drama to our festivals by electing a queen. We bestow a title on the queen according to what is being celebrated—Sugarcane Queen, Rice Queen, and let's not forget the Andouille (Sausage) Queen.

Outsiders may laugh at us, but visitors who attend these wonderful events all "pass a good time" with locals. The parades, festivals and celebrations in Louisiana are unlike anything they've ever experienced. Louisiana puts on the best parades in the world, not only for Mardi Gras, but also for other special occasions, such as religious feast days like Saint Joseph's Day. Participants generously give parade viewers lots of free "throws." Just about anything can be caught: bead necklaces, delicious Moon Pies, or even a cabbage from the St. Patrick's Day Parade. Royalty presented during a parade is much larger than that of a festival; an entire court of sovereigns, from King to Maids, are on view, dressed in lavish costumes. The celebration for each carnival group includes party-style meetings that lead up to a grand ball of monarchs, but just about anyone who wants to participate can become a member or buy a ticket for the masquerade. The parade is free of charge.

While rebuilding efforts were being made after Katrina's wrath, these familiar and loved traditions of Louisiana's culture were missed, especially among relocated evacuees. Refugees—who referred to themselves as "displaced"—longed to be reunited with family and reconnected with a familiar joie de vivre that lives in the heartland of Louisiana. Even sympathetic tourists wished to return to enjoy the many festivities. But no hardship, not even Katrina's strong winds, could blow away the life force of Louisiana's spirit; and so the spirit remained, waiting to bring healing to those who would return to mend their wounds.

Historians may disagree, but I believe this spirit was born in the year 1727, as New Orleans was in the initial stages of its life. In its infancy, the city's diverse cultures flourished, each contributing its own style of music, traditions, creative foods, and religious faith. But this very unique life force that has survived for hundreds of years would have never existed without those who helped build its foundation. They were selfless leaders, working not for personal gain, but for the greater good. These visionaries built a community with works of charity. They arrived in the U.S. through the mouth of the great mighty Mississippi River, entering one of the most important ports in our country, the Port of New Orleans. Their character was one of strength, perseverance and faith in God. They were a pillar of morality before governance had been established among newcomers who were flocking to the new world with various agendas. These missionaries' historical achievements would branch out further as they were the first to establish an orphanage, educate women, and manage a public hospital in the U.S. Who were they? Forget brave, tough men. They were nuns of the Ursuline order from France.

During their initial voyage, they courageously sailed rough seas, faced pirates, rationed food, and endured sickness as they journeyed to a land they had never seen. Confined to a small ship for eight months, twelve nuns crammed into one private quarter. Their hinged beds were wooden-planked bunks attached to the ship's crude walls. At night, they lay motionless within their restrictive quarters with only inches of space between each bed. The room's only ventilation was through two portals, each the size of two small hands.

Thrashing waves and storms often threw the ship about the seas. In their long, wool habits, they were often consumed by seasickness. What's worse, their faith was put to the test as they encountered pirate ships. As the ship's cannons prepared to blast, the nuns' only defense was prayers, prayers that rose quickly to heaven. They beseeched God not to let them sink and drown or to be captured and tortured. Heaven did answer their prayers, for they and the ship's crew escaped danger.

However, they faced even greater obstacles after their arrival, such as swamps, reptiles, mosquitoes, epidemics, and war. Those around them were in need of their charitable works though, whether it was providing food, shelter, or protection. The nuns would play a vital role in U.S. history by assisting Gen. Andrew Jackson and his soldiers during the War of 1812. These heroic nuns served as inspiring examples, setting the standard for each generation of Louisianians to emulate the nuns' resilience and ability to overcome hardships. Faith in God, hope, and charity was part of the formation of the Louisiana spirit. The nuns also have a historical connection to the Patroness of Louisiana, Our Lady of Prompt Succor, who is respected by many devotees, not only in Louisiana but throughout the South.

A request for another regional jewelry design compelled me to convey this connection that was representative of those first steps of faith taken by the Ursuline nuns. I knew I needed to conduct research. I found myself, two hundred eighty years after their arrival, knocking on the door of the convent in search of facts. I was greeted by Sister Damian who had a slight waddle to her walk. Her kind face radiated patience and love. Her eyes were a brilliant crystal blue, and I wondered about her past life. Her calming smile came from a faith that was uncompromising, as if she had laughed in the devil's face more than once. I explained that I was researching the history of intercessory prayers under the title of Our Lady of Prompt Succor, the Patroness of Louisiana. Grinning, Sister Damian invited me in and generously offered me a Coke. Through the convent doors, I entered a world that is foreign to this century, far from text messaging and satellites. I followed her out into a huge, tranquil courtyard that was surrounded by strong, high concrete walls that offered a retreat from the outside world. Without the daily city noise, my senses became heightened, taking delight in what I saw: gigantic old evergreens, palm trees and a pleasing landscape that has been maintained by gentle hands for many years. As we walked through this serene environment, I could easily visualize an image from an earlier period: nuns covered head to toe in black, meditating in deep prayer, reflecting on their work and the desire to connect to God's will. Sister Damian, still walking ahead of me, led me toward an old, wood screened door that softly squeaked as she opened it. I remained in the trance of a bygone day.

As I entered the room, my eyes lifted up toward the tall ceiling, and an inviting breeze from old wooden ceiling fans softly landed upon my face, soothing me and anyone else fortunate enough to gather beneath them. We talked and shared our Katrina stories. I told Sister Damian my thoughts of designing a piece of jewelry that would include our neighbors from the Gulf Coast region and all those in need. Patiently, she listened and waited for me to finish my Coke. Understanding the task at hand, she escorted me to a reference center where I was introduced to the archivist, Sister Joan Maria, who just happened to be Damian's sister by blood. They are from a large family in the River Parish, raised in a rural area located along the Mississippi River. Their upbringing is representative of their character: unafraid of commitment and hard work. They grew up knowing the value of life's laughter. They shared their history with me. Intrigued, I didn't want to leave. I had more curiosity than time.

Sister Damian asked, "Anne, would you like a copy of Andrew Jackson's letter?"

Delighted, I responded, "Yes."

Anne and Sister Damian Aycock, Order of Saint Ursula

I departed with a stack of books and a copy of Jackson's letter for my research.

During a period of the French Revolution, Catholics were forbidden to practice their faith, and some were tortured and put to death for public display. During that same period, Louisiana was transitioning from Spanish to French rule under Napoleon Bonaparte. The New Orleans Ursuline nuns of Spanish decent feared anti-clerical sentiments popularized by the French Revolution. Fleeing for safety, they left behind only a few French nuns to maintain their operations of charity. A nun, Mother St. Michel who lived in France, received a letter from her cousin, Mother Saint Andre Madier of New Orleans, requesting that sisters from France come to their aid. Sister Michel, wanting to offer assistance, went to her superior to request permission to leave France. She was denied. Her superior, Bishop Fournier, felt he could not afford to lose her to New Orleans. He hoped things would soon settle down in France where she would be needed to return to her charitable duties in her own community. Bishop Fournier told her that the only way she could go was if the Pope himself gave her permission to leave.

The year was 1809, and Pope Pius VII was incarcerated under the custody of Napoleon. Such permission was impossible to receive because communicating with the Pope was forbidden and he was to receive no visitors or mail. However, moved by faith, Mother Michel wrote a letter to the Pope while privately vowing that if she received a quick and favorable response, she would have the title of Our Lady of Prompt Succor venerated in New Orleans, Louisiana. Her letter miraculously made it into the hands of the Pope, and within one month, she received permission to leave for New Orleans. Grateful, she fulfilled her promise to have Our Lady of Prompt Succor honored.

Throughout history, many blessings have been bestowed to devotees, and Heaven's divine plans have shielded Louisiana and the United States from harm. Historically, Our Lady of Prompt Succor is associated with two significant and miraculous events: the great fire of New Orleans in 1812 that almost devastated all of the French Quarter and a prayerful intervention for the U.S. victory in the battle of New Orleans during the War of 1812.

In 1815, as the British were attempting to enter the United States through the mouth of the Mississippi River, General Andrew Jackson knew his troops were outnumbered 16,000 to his 6,000. Facing a shortage of ammunition and in need of additional support, Jackson reached out to the famous pirate Jean Lafitte and his men for military assistance. Jackson, a prayerful man, acknowledged the needed hand of God. Jackson went to visit Mother Marie Olivier de Vezin, the superior at the convent, to request the Ursulines' prayers for the safety of the troops and a successful mission. On the eve of the battle, January 8th, the faithful, including the wives and daughters of the American soldiers, joined the Ursuline nuns in their chapel as they petitioned Louisiana's patron for her prompt, motherly protection. Favorable occurrences quickly unfolded for the American soldiers. Strange manifestations caused the battle to end expeditiously, miraculously lasting only minutes. An unusually heavy fog covered the swampy battlefield, and the Brits quickly lost their bearings and became confused. They wandered about the marshy land in their bright red coats, making them easy targets. Heaven bestowed mercy on them, for they suffered few casualties, and most became prisoners of war. Jackson emerged victorious. Had this battle ended differently, the United States of America would not be what it is today.

After the battle, Jackson went to the convent and earnestly thanked the nuns for their prayers. He stated in a letter, "The unerring hand of Providence has shielded my men! By the blessing of heaven, directing the valor of the troops under my command, one of the most brilliant victories in the annals of war was obtained." The Ursulines resumed their works of charity, caring for the injured British soldiers and aiding them in their return home.

Motivated by the history and intrigued by the possibilities, I decided to write a letter to the Pope on behalf of the many Katrina victims. The odds of Pope Benedict XVI responding to my little note in this day and age seemed highly unlikely. Remarkably, one year later, almost to the day, I received correspondence from the Vatican Secretariat of State written on behalf of the Pope imparting an Apostolic Blessing. Let the blessings fall!

Inspired to help rekindle the spirit that embodies the people of Louisiana, I continued creating a collection of jewelry designs that were indicative of the region. The collection began with the most recognized and famous symbol of Louisiana, the fleur-de-lis. The three petals that make up the fleur-de-lis are representative of faith, wisdom, and chivalry—virtues needed as Katrina victims rebuilt. Fittingly, "The Signature Fleur-de-Lis™" pendant and earring design came to life. Next, was the "Return to New Orleans Ring™," a crest style, alameda, fleur-de-lis ring with an inscription of "Made in Louisiana" inlayed under the crown portion of the ring. People longed for such a collection of jewelry. It was embraced by enthusiasts of all things Louisiana.

Jim Belushi and wife, Jennifer Sloan, wearing the
"Return to New Orleans Ring©"

The collection reflects Louisiana's soul-filled culture and history as well as a traditional southern dish, Monday Red Beans. Red beans are a popular dinner that most everybody's mama makes on Monday. The tradition started before washing machines were invented. Monday was wash day, and it was a laborious process that required many hours. The first step was to soak the laundry in a galvanized tub the night before. The next morning, the clothes were scrubbed by hand on a washboard and then rinsed. Clothing that needed to be starched was placed into a cooking pot on the stove and then hung out to dry for ironing. Southern Creole Red Beans requires slow cooking, making it a perfect dish for wash day. Even today, after the invention of the modern washing machines, many Louisianians eat their red beans and rice on Monday. Thus, the "Monday Red Bean©" design was created, cast in the shape of a red bean to feature my New Orleans ancestors' recipe.

ANNE DALE

The famed tradition of the New Orleans Blessed Lucky Bean would also be incorporated into the collection. Its origin is from Sicilian Italian Catholics. New Orleans has always had a sizable Italian population. Immigrants from Sicily brought the tradition of celebrating the feast day of Saint Joseph by building an altar in their homes. When I was a little girl, every year around the feast day of March 19th, my na-nan would bring me to the French Quarter. Devotees would place a green branch above their doors to indicate that their altar was open to the public for viewing. Seeing an abundance of mouthwatering food, pasta, and cookies only made me hungry. My na-nan would ask, "Annie, are you saying your prayers?"

"Yes, I'm praying for that food."

When I got older, I started to host my own Saint Joseph Altar, feeding anyone who visited.

2012, Dad, mom and sisters. Left to right: Jennifer, Suzanne, Paul, Diane, Anne, Kay, and Dona in front of the Saint Joseph Altar held at the jewelry store. Dad is wearing his Honorary Grand Marshall medallion from the Italian American Marching Club

Since New Orleans is the birthplace of famed jazz, it was natural that I incorporate the city's and the state's unique musical tradition into this collection. The region has been very blessed with many gifted musicians, hailing from all over the world. Some of the first were the rhythmic dancers and drummers of the Congo. Later, in the nineteenth century, people of Italian descent played a prominent role as organ grinders. Similarly, New Orleans jazz appeals to many people around the world, drawing visitors to the place where it originated.

I was fortunate enough to be around all this music growing up. We lived close to a woman who was a retired New Orleans jazz singer and dancer. Every evening she would sit on the porch of her shotgun home, humming a tune. I hurried to do my chores so I could go outside to listen to her. Regularly, I would ask her, "Hey Ms. Josephine, what 'cha singing?"

"'Basin Street Blues,' precious."

"Precious" was how she addressed everyone.

"Man, Ms. Josephine you know a lot of tunes. Every day you've got a new one."

"Variety is the spice of life, precious. New Orleans music— ain't nuttin' like it in the warld. With de talent das born here, you'd sware somedin' waz in de air, de 'spirit' of music. Did I ever tell you I sang for . . . ?"

Ms. Josephine was delighted to share her many stories of how her path in life crossed with many musicians, some very famous. But I enjoyed her singing even more. The songs she sang came from her soul, and they carried me away as if I didn't have a care in the world. Breaking into one song after another, her voice was soothing. She sang not only jazz, but bluesy gospel songs that she claimed the Lord had taught her. They were songs that would make me want to drop to my knees and cry with a desire to see the splendor of God: "Sweet spirit (umm), oh sweet spirit—come for me, Jesus."

Was Ms. Josephine right? Is there a "music spirit" floating about in the air for gifting? Is that why so many New Orleans musicians become famous and influence the next generation to pick up an instrument?

My own father, born and raised in the ninth ward of New Orleans, was a gifted, world-renowned jazz drummer. At birth, he weighed only four pounds, and as he grew, he remained small in stature. When he was a little boy, he carried a stick for protection. At the age of seven, that music spirit, perhaps an "Angel of New Orleans," must have played a tempting tune for him. Walking home from school every day, he would run his stick along the many wrought-iron fences of New Orleans, producing what he thought to be a pleasurable sound for all the neighbors. One day, as he was clanking across the fences, to his surprise he heard something new, an echoing beat that vibrated differently. He had tapped his stick on a metal drum that was used to burn trash. The strange sound from the metal barrel sparked his interest. As he peered down into it, he saw a broken snare drum. It was there for the taking. Barely able to reach down into the barrel, determined, he struggled with all his might. Finally grabbing hold of the snare drum, he claimed it and took it home. He shined the drum's rim and fixed it as best he could. Did that Angel of New Orleans give him his first drum? My father, Paul Ferrara, was to be a drummer, and his heart beat to the sound of jazz music.

His noteworthy career included a list of performances on radio, television shows, and movies. He performed for four United States Presidents, Frank Sinatra, Billie Holiday, Dean Martin, Tommy Dorsey, Johnny Cash, and Ella Fitzgerald, just to name a few. He recorded with everyone from the jazzy Louis Prima to the big band leader Nelson Riddle. He also made records with one-of-a-kind musician Al Hirt and was included in the story of the evolution of jazz for National Geographic.

Appreciating the artfulness that collectively cultivated New Orleans, I wrote the following:

Return to New Orleans

Laissez Les Bons Temps Rouler

*Every great city has great food, music, festivals, and culture.
It's the same in New Orleans, only better, richer and
sweeter.*

*Return to New Orleans if you carry her—the Jewel of the
South, the Queen of Dixie—in your heart.*

*Return to New Orleans if you love to celebrate the world's
biggest party by raising your hands high in the air and
shouting "Throw me something mister; it's Mardi Gras!"*

*Return to New Orleans if you love to listen to blues, jazz,
or zydeco, and allow yourself to be transported into a
magical moment where time is no more.*

*Return to New Orleans, and gaze upon the city's beauty—
her French, Spanish, and Creole architecture, her southern
strength and nobility—where her graceful wrought-iron
designs whisper her culture.*

*Return to New Orleans, and tantalize your taste buds with
mouth-watering seafood, richly spiced dishes, and beignets.*

*Return to New Orleans, and you will refer to everyone as
"cher," where everything is "precious," where young people
acknowledge their elders by their first names preceded with
a polite "Mr." or "Ms.," where no one gossips, but "catches
up," and where everyone says, "Bless your heart" and means
it, in every conversation.*

*Return to New Orleans, visit when you can and stay
awhile. New Orleans . . . a city that truly knows how to
embrace life in a lagniappe (a little something extra) way.
It's what the city is all about, a city that wants to share its
joy with others.*

*No matter how long you're away, it will always be your
home, your favorite city, and your fondest memory. Once
experienced, it is a part of you, and a place your heart will
long for. Louisiana welcomes you and awaits your return.*

Katrina victims began to heal as they rebuilt and reunited with family and friends. They became reacquainted with the spirit of Louisiana. Many areas of the affected region improved financially through donations, insurance settlements, and tax credits. Rebuilding had an incredible domino effect on the local economy, and employment picked up. Tradesmen and laborers had more work than they could handle; many had to hire additional workers. From furniture stores and hotels to local restaurants, many businesses flourished. From contractors and electricians to plumbers and landscapers, people flocked into the city. Months after the storm, blessings fell from heaven.

CHAPTER 16

Jeweler for a Cause®

Inspired Blessings

The "Self-Esteem©" jewelry design

The jewelry store and Louisiana collection thrived. I was grateful for every sale, but in the back of my mind, I realized I had no extra time to promote gemological education in the U.S. The bittersweet reality that I had to make a career decision set in. My dream to further gemological education in the U.S. came to an end, at least temporarily. So I flew to London with my lucky stone to turn in my resignation, face to face. In 2005, I resigned from the Gemological Association and from Gem-A USA.

With mixed emotions, I said my goodbyes to my fellow gemologists, and I left London with a heavy heart. Although I felt a void, something inside of me knew my journey with gems was not over. To pass time while waiting at the plane's gate for my flight back to the States, I people watched. Surfing the many faces in the terminal, I saw in the not-too-far distance a maintenance man carefully sweeping. He must have sensed my mindless stare when through the crowd he suddenly raised his head towards me and smiled. His reaction struck me as odd, and immediately the blind broom man entered my mind. My insecure thoughts began searching, reaching for assurance that my resignation was the right decision. Anxious about the continued growth and development of the business back home, I wanted to believe that the sweeping man was a sign from heaven above not to worry. Now that I had made the decision to put all my efforts into the jewelry store, I desperately wanted affirmation. I wanted him to signify that opportunity would continue to guide me, that the jewelry store would always sustain us and continue to evolve. But what was the next step, and when would we take it, I wondered?

I was still in deep thought as I boarded, shuffling onto the plane, when a woman noticed the pendant I was wearing. Pointing to my necklace, she asked, "Where did you get that?"

Before I could answer, she stated, "I love music."

I was wearing the "Rhythm of Louisiana" pendant. "I made it," I said. "I have a jewelry store in Louisiana, and this is part of a collection I created."

"I am a 'wanna-be' musician," she proclaimed.

"Me too," I said as I handed her my business card.

She continued, "Which means I try. I can't sing or play an instrument, but if I had known what I know today, I would have followed my dream of being a musician."

"Hey, it's never too late . . . What do you do for a living?" I asked.

"I'm a sign language interpreter for the hearing impaired."

"Wow, that's cool! . . . I guess you could say you are a musician; you play music with your hands."

"Thanks, I never thought of it that way . . . My daughter inherited my love for music. She plays the violin. I encourage her every chance I get. I'd like to get her one of those music pendants. Can I order them online?"

As I settled into my seat, I was struck with a flow of synchronized thoughts that played in my mind, and I froze. The image of the man smiling and sweeping and of the woman who was an interpreter for the deaf replayed in my mind, as did the way she expressed her passion, her interest, and her daughter's interest all because of the pendant. All thoughts suddenly formed an entrepreneurial seizure, an idea, an opportunity. Realizing I truly was on the brink of something incredible, I didn't want to move, afraid of losing those thoughts in motion. As the plane took off, I stared into the endless sky, wishing for more clarity. Knowing that the blind broom man always inspired me, I beckoned him to knock on my imaginary door. And there he stood with the weighty brooms resting upon his shoulder.

Opening the door, I impatiently asked, "What, what, please tell me what does all this mean?"

With a blunt but kind tone, he asked, "Anne, how do I hear?"

His ghostlike manifestation seemed so real to me that even when I answered him in my head, I had to stop myself from actually shrugging my shoulders on the plane.

"With your ears," I said.

"How do I see?"

Pausing in thought before answering, I said, "With your ears, too . . . your hearing."

Then he asked, "Tell me a way in which people with sight listen?"

Suddenly, I was enlightened, replying, "People hear what they see . . . I got it, thank you!"

How true: people hear what they see, whether they are hearing impaired or not. Imagery is a language with an endless vocabulary. Astonished, I realized a revolutionary concept that the jewelry trade had not embarked on. Beyond the celebration of love between a couple or among family members, the industry offered no "real" jewelry— jewelry that is crafted with precious metals, unlike costume jewelry—that expressed other human passions or storms in life. No other "real" jewelry communicated a desire to fulfill dreams, ambitions, offer encouragement, or be supportive in the face of human challenges.

As the design ideas whirled around in my head, I knew the concept could connect a multitude of people who have weathered, and will weather, the storms of life. Such jewelry would allow people to express their own personalities and passions in a way conventional t-shirts, tattoos, and body piercings cannot. The creation of this jewelry collection would voice optimism—the saving grace in life's storm—as well as inspire, encourage and support people.

I found it perplexing that no one in the jewelry trade had yet realized the possibilities of this unique concept. Sure, precious metal logo pins, award jewelry, and watches were available to a few select club members or personnel employed for a certain number of years. The only segmented jewelry that even comes close to embracing this concept are graduation rings, sports emblems, and faith-based pieces. Still, no "real jewelry" existed that truly reflected shared human emotions, desires, or challenges. There was much more to the heart of a person waiting to be captured that we as a society collectively value and share.

The moment of discovery manifested itself as a gift that was being handed to me, a responsibility to make the most of this unclaimed territory in the industry. Looking forward, the task of creating a category of jewelry with no precedent in the market would be huge and time consuming. Nevertheless, I was committed, knowing that the results of this endeavor would mean so much to so many.

Immediately, I began sketching designs from my cramped seat on the plane, all the while gazing out the window into the heavens for inspiration. Jewelry for a Cause® was created. I envisioned this jewelry collection to visually shout encouragement, motivation, and perseverance, and to bring about an awareness of the challenges faced by people from all walks of life. I soon realized that the people in my life—young and old, healthy and disabled—would provide the motivation I needed to set out on this new journey.

— § —

One of the first designs, and very dear to my heart was inspired by my three children. Besides their decent grades, they have talents that Mike and I never dreamed of possessing. They are admirable young people who set goals and possess a confidence that anything is attainable if they set their minds to it. Each of my children's dreams are big: Grace a psychologist or lawyer; Paul a film producer and writer; and Stephen a singer or business owner.

Paul, Grace, and Stephen Dale

As the collection developed, I sought insight from their youthful perspective. I asked them to share their thoughts on what mattered in life, what made them feel valued, and what they defined as success. Each offered the same basic answers—God, integrity, and confidence. Out of these values, I created the "Self-Esteem©" jewelry design.

It is important that every adolescent's self-esteem is nurtured. Valuable support can come from parents, friends, teachers, coaches, and many others. A critical turning point in discovering one's self-worth for most young people comes with the realization that their life has purpose. For Stephen, my oldest, this turning point came early, requiring confidence and maturity beyond his years.

The moment Stephen was born, he gasped for the air of this world and then let out an incredibly loud, healthy cry. His lungs were powerful and his voice was music to my ears. He let everyone know he had arrived. As I lay in the hospital bed, the doctor held him up high for me to get my first look at him.

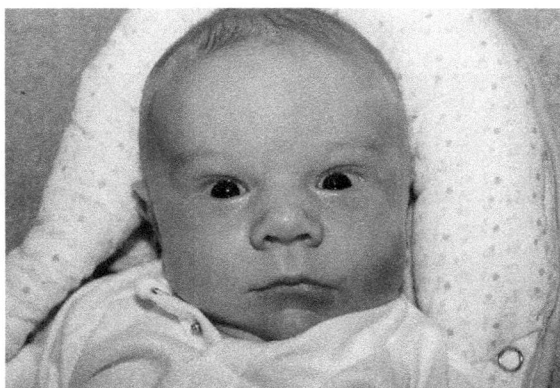

Stephen Dale, "Look out world, I'm here."

To keep him warm, the nurse placed a cap on his head and bundled him snug in a blanket. With love and open arms, I reached for my son. I watched his bottom lip quiver as he quieted down to the sound of my voice. I was in awe of this beautiful human being, and I thanked God for him.

Stephen was born with a port-wine birthmark on the left side of his face. Mike and I didn't think much of it; all we saw was the miracle of Stephen. I endured numerous complications during my pregnancy with him. At times, it looked doubtful that I would carry him to term. So after much pain-staking bed rest, Mike and

I were delighted with the birth of a pudgy, healthy, eight-pound thirteen-ounce beautiful baby. We were proud parents.

Within a couple hours of Stephen's birth, the pediatrician came into the hospital room to talk with us about Stephen's port-wine stain. Because of its location, a CAT scan of Stephen's head was necessary to make certain there were no underlying issues. The results came back normal, but as a precaution, the doctor advised us that Stephen's birthmark should be evaluated by a specialist.

Stephen, a healthy baby, grew quickly, eating everything in sight. We did our research, trying our best to stay abreast of any health risks related to his port-wine stain. Complications from thickening blood vessels, which could cause bleeding, were a real possibility with Stephen's condition. Meanwhile, we brought Stephen to a dermatologist who informed us our baby boy would need continuous preventative laser treatments—the sooner we got started, the better. At two months old, he underwent his first procedure. Because the laser treatments would likely cause him great pain, we opted for general anesthesia. The doctor's cautionary words—"the possibility of complications resulting in death"—gave me pause and resonated in my heart.

After each treatment, I could smell his burned skin. It was a distinctive smell that made me mentally and physically hurt for Stephen. Slowly, as the years passed, new laser techniques were developed, but they too carried risks. And now, twenty years later, such treatments continue to have side effects and limitations. Today, when Stephen receives his laser treatment, he chooses not to be put to sleep, embracing the stinging, burning laser that emits a beam of six to seven millimeters in diameter as many as 650 times in one treatment. Who would have thought that a birthmark could cause someone such concern and discomfort?

In addition to our concerns for Stephen's health, we worried about his self-esteem. Adults and kids would occasionally make rude statements and ask hurtful questions, as if Stephen couldn't be affected by them. From the time he was a small child, Mike and

I empowered him by allowing Stephen to respond directly to the inquirer. If he felt that he didn't want to respond to a statement or question, he could ignore it, and we did not answer for him. Many times I recall turning to Stephen and asking, "Do you want to answer the man?" Now and again Stephen would test the boundaries of his power, replying with a simple "no," and we would just remain silent and go about our business. Occasionally, people stood there dumbfounded because they were being ignored. They had become the focus. But when he did answer someone, he would often give a response with confidence, such as, "That's where the angel kissed me." As he got older, he responded with even greater assurance, stating, "That's my mark of greatness."

Stephen gained wisdom and matured with a healthy attitude, and his birthmark lost its relevance. As a handsome, charming young man, he possessed poise and confidence, ready to run toward the stage of life. And indeed, incredible events and opportunities began to unfold and further shape his already wonderful character.

Stephen is naturally gifted in music, and at fifteen, Stephen was accepted into the school of NOCCA, the New Orleans Center for Creative Arts. A year later, he began the Stephen Dale Project, which offers encouragement to others who might have something different about themselves. Barely old enough to drive, he became an inspirational guest speaker for a variety of organizations, especially youth groups, sharing his challenges—and more importantly, his positive attitude. Below is a portion of one of his presentations:

> I was born with a mark of greatness. My mark of greatness is what has made me who I am today. My name is Stephen Dale, and I have a port-wine birthmark on the left side of my face. While growing up, kids sometimes made fun, people stared, or they would make comments and asked questions.

When I was very young, my parents would empower me by allowing me to answer people who asked about my birthmark. If I didn't want to answer, I didn't, nor would my parents. That was one thing I could control; I had that power. When you have something different about yourself, you have to manage your reaction to people, and you have to do it every single day. The stares can often make you feel self-conscious about being pre-judged. Having to overcome such challenges has made me want to work harder at most things. My parents always taught me that I could be whatever I wanted to be. They not only said it, they believed it, and they believed in me.

Every once in a while, we all need to take an inventory of ourselves, of the stuff that is on the inside, and take an oath as to who we really are. This is my message—we have always heard "Don't judge a book by its cover." Stand on your own; you don't need society to tell you what you are supposed to look like. No matter what others may say or think, only you can control your content. That content is the stuff that is really important, the right stuff that is within you. It is true for everyone, whether you look or feel different. Develop your self-esteem and pursue your dreams. If you are wondering where my mark of greatness is . . . it's inside of me.

To end his presentation, he would sing a song. His natural stage presence and baritone voice echoed his boyhood desire of becoming a professional performer. Stephen would soon encounter an opportunity that would move him closer to realizing that dream.

Stephen and I were in New York for one of his laser treatments, and while there, we went to see *The Phantom of the Opera* on Broadway. He had been a fan of the musical since first seeing it at the age of twelve at the Saenger Theater in New Orleans, immediately becoming mesmerized by the Phantom. In fact, it was the performer who played the opera ghost who had inspired Stephen to begin vocal training in the first place. But tonight, with a few more years and much more confidence, he wanted to get a closer look at the Phantom.

"Mom," he asked, "do you think if I ask the doorman for a backstage tour he would let me?"

"Stephen, don't be afraid of 'no'. Go and ask."

The doorman saw Stephen's enthusiasm, offering him even more than what he asked for and inviting him to meet the performer who played the Phantom after the show. For Stephen, the performance could not end fast enough. Neither one of us had ever been backstage at a Broadway musical. After the curtain closed and the crowd left, we stood waiting in the big, empty, plush, and now quiet theater. The doorman motioned to us from across the auditorium and hurried us through the backstage area. He escorted us down a small hallway, a maze-like hallway that seemed to wind endlessly around the side stage, overflowing with costume racks and stage props. Our anticipation grew as we climbed up a narrow staircase where several small dressing rooms were located. On the outside of some of the doors were the performers' names. The dressing room door belonging to the Phantom read "Gary Mauer." My heart beat with excitement for Stephen. Our escort knocked, and the door slowly opened—there sat the Phantom having his makeup removed.

Mr. Mauer was incredibly welcoming. I could tell that Stephen was bursting at the seams but trying to play it cool in front of the much-celebrated actor. Mr. Mauer graciously took his time showing us around—a personal backstage tour by the Phantom performer himself. The sound of our echoing footsteps could be heard as he led us across the huge stage floor. Stephen stopped and stood smack dab in the center. Pausing, he faced the theater's empty seats, and his face lit up with the youthful rays of future dreams. I knew what Stephen was thinking. As Mr. Mauer graciously continued the tour and pointed out more props, I leaned over and whispered in Stephen's ear: "Stephen, you will be here one day. How does it feel?" He slowly turned to me and nodded. Speaking with only his eyes, he smiled.

Backstage with Gary Mauer, "The Phantom of the Opera"

That evening in New York, Stephen soared with thoughts of a successful future in voice and on Broadway. He stayed in touch with Mr. Mauer and every time we went back to the Big Apple for a doctor visit, Stephen went to see the musical *The Phantom of the Opera.*

Soon, fate would bring Stephen and Mr. Mauer together again in another special way. Stephen was involved with a charitable organization and asked the actor if he would perform with him at a fundraiser in New York City. There, Stephen stood by his mentor and sang. For Stephen, the experience would further drive his ambition to pursue his dream.

At eighteen, Stephen decided to travel to New York City alone. Without being a Broadway Equity Card holder, he and hundreds of other aspiring performers auditioned for the Phantom of the Opera Company. Arriving very early to the audition, he was happy to receive call number 186, well ahead of many of the other non-union performers present. Stephen anxiously hung about the hallways for hours, waiting for his chance. All too soon, whispers of disappointment among those who were waiting passed down the corridor; the panel of judges would not have time to see auditions from non-union performers, and many started to leave.

Stephen Dale and Gary Mauer singing together for a
fundraiser at the Hudson Theater in New York

Disheartened but determined, Stephen was not ready to accept "No." Turning toward the audition door, he just walked right in. "No one stopped me, so I went all the way in," he said, relaying his story. "Hello, my name is Stephen Dale. I am from Louisiana. I was born to play the Phantom. They let me talk, and so I did. One of the judges stood up, came from around the desk at which she sat, hugged and kissed me. 'You are so real,' she said. They told me they would allow me to sing for them only after union auditions ended. They said they would call me on my cell phone when they were ready for me. Not taking any chances, I waited nearby. Not wanting to miss the opportunity, I planted myself in the lobby of the building in a chair between the elevator and the exit door. Five o'clock came, and the security guard informed me that the building would be closing and that I would have to leave. At that moment, the elevator door opened and a woman stepped out inquiring if I was Stephen Dale. I jumped up and replied, 'Yes!'

She said, 'They are ready for you.' I walked in, handed the piano player my sheet music, and began singing 'Stars' from the musical Les Miserable. I think they were surprised that I could really sing. Then they asked me to sing again. I sang three songs. They asked questions about me. I grew excited as the conversation seemed to indicate they were considering me for the role. 'How old are you?' they asked. 'Eighteen,' I told them. Suddenly, all got quiet, and I didn't understand why. I asked, 'What—what?' Simultaneously, the panel of judges responded, 'You're too young. You have to be at least twenty-one years old.' Disappointed, I said 'That's three years from now; I might decide to do something else when I am twenty-one.' They were encouraging. Confidently, one replied, 'No you won't; you'll be working here.' They encouraged me to finish college, continue my studies in music, and stay in touch. Two of the judges gave me their contact information, cell numbers and emails, so that I could keep in touch. It was a stressful, long day, but for twenty glorious minutes, I had a captive audience of those who decide who will be the Phantom, and in audition time that is miraculous."

As Stephen demonstrates, it is not about how we "think" others see us, but, ultimately, how we define ourselves. He was the inspiration for me to write the following:

Self-Esteem

I Believe...

I believe beauty comes from within.

I believe in God, His creation, and that I am truly unique and special.

I believe in making the best use of the gifts I was born with.

I believe in integrity, discipline and respecting myself and others.

I believe true success will come to me when I work hard and persevere at my goals.

I believe a positive and loving attitude is true beauty, and it comes from within.

The "Jewelry For a Cause®" collection was successfully fulfilling a need for many people. I added more designs to the collection such as "Facing Autism," "Perseverance" for cancer, "Rising Star" for hope, and "The Power of One" for inspiration. Customers purchased the pieces in pendants, pins and bracelets, as they express their feelings of support for a specific cause or group of people. Their purchases help inspire others and serve as outward displays of support and appreciation. The collection compels customers to heartedly share their feelings and extraordinary stories—stories of real champions and heroes living among us.

Power of One Pendant© Perseverance Pendant© Facing Autism©

Katie Brewster: a "Crowning Moment™" Champion

Katie Brewster is one such champion whose life and message are exemplary. Her compelling story began at an annual high-school event where she took center stage and proclaimed to the world, "That which makes you different makes you beautiful." She's a leader who changed the world's perception of those with special needs.

Fontainebleau High School in Mandeville, Louisiana is home to two thousand students. On the night of October 3, 2009, the faithful Bulldog fans packed the stadium for their annual homecoming football game. Louisiana's unpredictable weather brought down a drenching rain on all who attended. However, football players and fans, full of school spirit, refused to let the downpour put a damper on their special event. Anxiously, the soaked student body waited for the half-time announcement revealing who would be their new homecoming queen. Hovering under umbrellas was a court of ten girls, each hoping that her name would be called. The anticipation was building as the announcer shared a bit about each girl's background and future plans over the sound of the crowd's applause. Wanting to be close to her daughter as the announcement was made, the proud mother of one of the candidates ran down from the stands to the fence that surrounded the playing field. Finally the moment arrived, and the high-school principal proudly announced the year's homecoming queen.

"Fontainebleau High, your 2009 homecoming queen, as elected by the student body, is . . . Katie Brewster!"

Michelle Anderson, the mother whose hands were clenched tightly to the wet steel fence, recalled that moment:

> When I heard my daughter's name called, I heard the crowd erupt, and my knees buckled. With tears streaming down my face, I watched her as she was handed a bouquet of roses and a crown was placed on her head. You see, my daughter has cerebral palsy. As she stood there among her peers, the stadium went into a total frenzy, my heart was exploding, Katie beamed, and the student body from up in the stands began cheering her name, "Katie, Katie, Katie!"

The "forgotten race" is how Katie's mother describes those who are sometimes overlooked and who long to be included in society. As society has slowly embraced members of the "forgotten race", a new era of understanding and acceptance has taken root.

"It was that moment that Katie felt the sense of truly belonging, of being valued and celebrated in spite of her disability," said Katie's mother, describing the evening her daughter was elected homecoming queen.

Ms. Katie Brewster, 2009

From early on in life, Katie has been a goal-setter with the stamina of an Olympic gold medalist. She has endured numerous surgeries, battled seizures, and fought a variety of orthopedic issues. Driven to succeed, Katie removed "I can't" from her vocabulary at an early age. Embracing patience, it would take her seven years to learn how to walk. Although she is non-verbal, she has mastered adaptive sign language. She does not welcome pity—only dignity and respect. Katie socially and physically pushes herself, choosing to be involved in as many activities as possible. This includes being an ambassador for Louisiana Easter Seals. Katie has never met a stranger, and her inner strength is unlike anything of this world.

Settling into an interview with Katie, before a word was spoken or a question asked, I discovered something profound about her. She captivated me the moment our eyes met.

Holding my attention, I sensed her amazing ability to look straight through me and discern my intent. Surprised and filled with awe, I could only stare back and grin. I was at a loss for words. She has a supernatural gift, an ability to see people for who they are, not how they want to be perceived. Much like an angel from the heavens, she too can see people for the unique creations they are. She sees truth. Humbled, I nodded my head in gratitude, appreciating her trust and confidence. To the outside world, our enchanted exchange of understanding lasted only seconds, but for me, it remains etched on my soul and will last a lifetime.

"Katie, what is your disability?" I asked.

"Cerebral palsy," her mother said, interpreting her sign language.

"What is your ability?"

"People. I am very social. I like people. I like to help people no matter who they are. I help care for others by doing things like pushing other students in their wheelchairs. I even help the school cheerleaders paint banners. I have a lot of energy and I like to go, go, and go. I like to keep busy with people and do things for them."

"What do you want others to know about people with disabilities?"

"That they are not defined by their disability. They have hopes and dreams. They have feelings."

"What advice would you give to special-needs young adults?" I asked.

"Some people see differences and need to overcome that behavior. So don't be afraid to get involved. For every four people who walk by you, one will reach out. Always hold your head up. Don't let other people's ignorance get you down. Remember, that which makes you different makes you beautiful."

"Crowning Moments©"

Moments of measure that
represent your best. Whether
in work or character you
achieve success. Now
placed upon your heart a
Crown shall rest.

A champion knows that in tragedy there is triumph, in suffering there is hope, and in pain there is resurrection.

Sometimes champions are called to wear a crown on their heart for others. Sometimes those champions are called into the storm, called to defend the freedom we often take for granted. Guardians for America are heroes that weather the storms for others.

CHAPTER 17

Lieutenant Colonel Oliver North
and Corporal Matt Cole

American Guardians

Marine Corporal Matthew Cole, 2000

Americans have a great appreciation for the Founding Fathers and for those who serve to protect our country's freedoms. My desire to show America's support and love for those guardians manifested itself in a jewelry design I titled "Star of Hope.™" It is a five-point star that represents the five branches of the military. Wrapped around the star is a ribbon tied in a bow, symbolizing a perpetual prayer for our protectors' safe-keeping during their missions.

When conversing with a military guardian, they never boast or exhibit an arrogant attitude. And although they are from different places and families, they all seem to share similar character traits. Such were the admirable attributes I found when meeting Corporal Matthew Cole for the first time. He exuded humility and exceptional heroic qualities. I asked him to share his spell-binding story. This is his recollection . . .

— § —

I grew up very patriotic. As soon as I graduated from high school, I joined the Marine Corps. The year was 1999, and all was right in the world of an eighteen year old. The history of America gave me no doubt that one day I would go to war. That knowledge became a sobering reality after 9-11. I participated in the invasion and liberation of Iraq. I came home proud of what we had accomplished, and I had great hope for the people of Iraq. The war continued, and I was deployed again in 2005. I was sent to Haditha, al-Anbar province. One quiet morning, three months into the deployment, we were preparing for an armored patrol when we were hit with mortars and rockets. The first mortar to drop exploded behind me, thrusting me fifteen feet and scattering shrapnel throughout my back. I lay there, on the ground, unable to feel or move my legs. I was dragged to safety, and I then realized that I could not breathe. Shrapnel had torn through my right lung, causing it to collapse. The corpsman on the scene, whom I credit with saving my life, informed me of my injuries and did the best he could to stop the bleeding and aid my breathing. Three Marines and the corpsman raced me and the other injured men to the medical aid station for further treatment. I was lying on a gurney, fighting for my life, when the battalion chaplain stood over me and gave me my last rites. It took an hour for the Medivac chopper to arrive. I took my first ride in a helicopter laid out on a gurney, fighting to breathe, and the thing that angered me most was the fact that I could not roll over and look out the window! I made it to the hospital, and they put me out. I awoke four days later stateside at the Bethesda Naval Hospital.

A few months ago, I received a letter from the corpsman that first treated me. It read:

Dear Matt,
I am sure you have no idea who I am. We have only spent 45 minutes of our lives together. I will tell you though, that I have revis-

ited those 45 minutes every single day since May 17th, 2005.

My name is Taylor Cleveland. I was a corpsman for 3/25 who served with you at the Dam in Haditha. I was the person who took care of you after you were wounded. It has taken me almost two years to find a way to contact you . . . and another two months to fight through the tears to write these first two paragraphs. I hope that by writing you I am not opening wounds that you have been fighting to heal. I just wanted to thank you for what you did for me that day. Because you see, the day you were wounded you saved my life.

On the 17th, I was on duty at the BAS. I had been assigned as a corpsman with K-Bar 10, but had been moved to the BAS after the ambush at the Haditha Hospital with K-Bar 7 on Mother's Day. The ambush left me recovering from a host of wounds, not the least of which were mental. That ambush took the life of my best friend, Jeff Wiener, Corpsman for K-Bar 7. My MAP team was sent as the QRF to rescue him and the other Marines, but Jeff died before I was able to get to him.

That guilt and a nasty staph infection from a booby trap at the hospital kept me working in the BAS for a bit while I recovered. I was running on the top of the Dam when your tracks got hit. After I heard the impacts, I ran straight to the BAS. One of the corpsmen was yelling, "Tracks just got hit hard!" I grabbed the first medical bag I found lying around and ran down the ramp to tracks in tennis shoes and my PT shorts. That was the first time we met. This is what I remember about the day.

When I got there the first thing I saw was your friend who ended up losing his arm. I never knew his name. I started to move to him when one of the other trackers grabbed me and yelled, "Doc, over here!" You were lying on the ramp of one of the tracks, face down, as gray as a thunder cloud, and breathing so shallowly that you might as well not have been.

I could see that the mortar round made a fist-sized hole in your back that had left you with a serious open chest wound. I opened the med kit to grab a chest seal and you guessed it . . . no chest seal . . . no occlusive dressing, nothing to help you. I yelled at one of your Marines to grab some duct tape, and that's how I patched the hole in your back . . . with 100mph tape.

I rolled you over and saw your face . . . you didn't look good. The chest wound had caused air to be trapped in your chest cavity instead of in your lungs. I needed to put a needle in your chest to let the air out so you could breathe. I tore through the med kit trying to find the needle that we use to do this, but . . . no needle either. All we had were IV needles and they were way too short to do what I needed to do.

I remember I started to swear about who put the med kit together. I remember trying to figure out how to help you with no supplies. I remember looking up at your Marines who I'm sure were thinking,"Great, we got the shitty Doc."

With no other choice, I had to put an IV needle in your chest to let the air out. But to get it in the right place I had to press down so hard I was almost standing on you. It worked a bit. Air came out and you started to breathe with a bit more purpose. You were better, but not good. I had to put a needle in your other side. This time you were a bit more conscious. That had the unfortunate effect of letting you feel me place this one. God, I felt so bad for how much that must have hurt. I could see your pain as you looked at me . . . but you didn't say a word.

The second needle made you able to breathe a bit better, you had improved from gray to pale and you were even moving your arms now. You were better, but not out of the woods. The needle decompression would only last a few minutes. In order to give you a chance to live, we needed to get you to the BAS and put a tube in your chest.

I remember telling one of your Marines that I needed a Humvee to get you to the BAS. All we could find was a four-seater with a four-foot pickup truck bed, not long enough to put you in. But put you in we did. Your back side was squarely on the tail gate, which was down, and two Marines were holding you by your belt. I was straddling you in order to be able to keep putting needles in your chest if I had to.

We drove that awful drive out the front gate and up to the 10th deck at about 60 mph. Halfway there, the frigging tailgate broke under the weight of you, me, and the only thing left was the two Marines holding both of us. There we were driving 60 mph up a mountain with both our legs bouncing off the ground.

I had to put two more needles in your chest as we drove. I knew it hurt, but I just had to. When I put the last one in you grabbed my hand as it was on your chest. I thought you were trying to pull the needle out because it hurt so badly. I yelled at you, telling you that I had to do this so you could breathe better; that I had to do this so you could live.

Then one of the Marines who was holding us in the truck told me in one of those voices that was so calm and quiet that it stuck out from all the yelling and noise going on around us. He said, "Doc, he just wants to hold your hand."

I was terrified. I was so scared that you were going to die. I just started yelling "NO! NO! Give me five minutes. If you can stay alive for five minutes. We can put a chest tube in you and you'll be fine. PLEASE give me five minutes." I begged you all the way to the BAS not to give up.

That's what sticks in my mind to this day. All my years of medical training, everything I had done to prepare for this moment . . . and all I could do is beg you not to die. I felt so helpless. I still feel helpless when I think about it.

But you didn't die. You held out for five minutes. We did get a chest tube in you. I remember looking at you as we put you in the helicopter. I told you that once you got to Al-Asad, they would get you into surgery, and you would be fine; that you just needed to hold on until then.

That was the last time I saw you. After that day, I had a long talk with God. After the ambush in Haditha, I wasn't sure what purpose I was serving being here if I couldn't help anyone. After you, I felt more at peace. Like you were the purpose for me being there, like I had done what I came to Iraq to do.

Our whole BAS was pulling for you. It was like a win after losing so many guys on Mother's Day. A few days later, our casualty tracker broke some news to us at our briefing. He said that you were in Germany and were not going to make it; that they didn't expect you to live through the day.

I broke down crying. The whole day I spent in my room crying, angry with myself, with God, with the war. Why had I been allowed to help you, only for you to die later? Why do everywhere I go, Marines just keep dying? Why . . . ?

Matt went on to say:

In the letter, he explained that when they put me on the Medivac, it was understood that I likely would not make it to the hospital. The first hospital did not have the ability to treat my injuries, so they shipped me to a main hospital in Iraq. However, that hospital did not have a doctor specializing in lung injuries. Laying on a gurney in the hospital hallway, a priest anointed the sacrament of the sick (my last rite). I realized I was bad off, I prayed, "I love you God, I love you. God . . . I don't want to die." At that moment, standing over me appeared a Navy reservist CB who just happened to be passing through the hospital. Miraculously, he was a lung specialist and surgeon in the civilian world. That, to me, is hope.

The corpsman's letter continues:

Days later we found out that you didn't die, and that you were sent to the states. That was like a 1,000 lb weight that was lifted off of my chest. I felt better. I felt I had purpose again. I felt ready to get back to war.

I really feel that God never gives us any more then we can handle. He knew what I could handle in Iraq and he gave it to me.

I told you earlier that you saved my life, and that's just what I meant. If you had died holding my hand in the middle of that desert, my life would have been over. I never would have emotionally or psychologically been able to recover from that. That would have been more than I could handle. I would have been another casualty of war. I may have made it home, but the life, the home, and the family that I have been blessed with saved me from that. You lived. Because of your strength, your determination, and unwavering intrepidity, you lived. And doing so, you allowed me to keep living.

Thank you, Matt. Thank you for the life I have today, and all you have given up so that I could have it. If there is ever anything that I can do for you, or your family, I would be honored.

Semper Fi,
Taylor "Doc" Cleveland

*Medical Corpsman
Taylor "Doc" Cleveland*

Corporal Matthew Cole

Corporal Matthew Cole is a hero. Paralyzed from the chest down, he defeated death and is grateful to be alive. He wears his Marine persona inside and out. Even when he is in his civilian clothing, only briefly one might see a wheelchair but within seconds you see the quantifiable substance that earned him his Purple Heart. His story, his presence, his life, his great sacrifice, reminds people that America's freedom is a privilege that is earned, a treasured gift that must be guarded and respected. Matt never ceases to serve. On October 10, 2010, Matt Cole crossed a threshold to help change medical history. He is the first person in the country to participate in the U.S. Food and Drug Administration's adult stem-cell clinical trial (not from aborted fetal tissue) to treat spinal cord injuries, under the care of Dr. Gabriel Lasala. Matt knows he is doing this for more people than himself.

"I hope what they can learn from me can help everyone and may be available for insurance coverage at the VA. Everyone that lives in a chair wants to get out of it. I want to be the one that proves the doctors wrong," he said.

Today Matt works as an officer representing Veterans of War. He and his wife Kim have three beautiful children.

Thank you Corporal Matthew Cole for you selfless service.

Star of Hope©

The "Star of Hope" jewelry design would reach another note-worthy hero. On November 6th, 2008, I was invited to present and address soldiers who were being honored for their military service through a nonprofit organization, Support Our War Heroes. Their annual event, "In the Company of Heroes," was being held at the WWII D-Day Museum in New Orleans with five hundred antici-pated attendees. The guest speaker was retired Lieutenant Colonel Oliver North. I had the honor to present and pin him with the "Star of Hope."

At a loss for words with which to express the enormous grati-tude I felt towards the soldiers, I began my presentation:

> Thank you. It is an honor and I am humbled by the heroes and their families here tonight. When I was a little girl, I entered an essay contest on "Why I Am Proud to be an American." I wrote about the streets in America being paved with golden opportunities. I wrote about freedom—the right to express my beliefs and the freedom to practice my faith in God. Today my views remain steadfast, and I am always hopeful about America.

The United States of America has been through times of disappointments, depressions, wars, peace, under poor leadership, and under great leadership. And through all of this, we never waiver from hope, especially in our military and among Americans who hold strong patriotic beliefs in the depths of their hearts. You, the military, guardians of our country, are why America is the land of opportunity, the land of freedom, and the most charitable of all nations in the world.

Reflecting on the heroes here tonight, I would like to share this thought with those of us who are not in the military. I know that in a heartbeat I would give my life for my children, but how many of us would have the courage to sacrifice our lives for our neighbor, or for generations to come—generations of people who we will never meet?

Guardians, you sacrifice your one life, the only life you get in this world, for an incredible and higher understanding; you have a greater love for our country and fellow Americans.

Today it is important that each and every one of us carry the message of how and why we are where we are today. It's because of the men and women who serve our country.

I, we, honor and support you.

It is for this reason I designed the Star of Hope. I took what I could offer, my God-given talent, to try to say all this in the best way I knew how, and I ask others to share in expressing their support and honor by wearing the Star of Hope.

Then it came time to address Oliver North. The distinguished, retired, decorated Marine officer has been awarded for his service with a Silver Star, the Bronze Star for valor, and two Purple Hearts. He was assigned to the National Security Council during the 1980s, when President Ronald Reagan acknowledged him as an American Hero. His life accomplishments continue today as an author, syndicated columnist, host of the award-winning Fox News Channel documentary series "War Heroes," and honorary chairman of Freedom Alliance.

I tried very hard not to appear nervous. In preparing my presentation, I scribbled notes all over my speech with big spaces, dark commas, and purposely misspelled words written boldly and spelled phonetically so I would not mispronounce them. By the looks of my paper, I could only imagine that Colonel North would probably take me for an idiot. The pressure was on. Trying to remain confident, I reminded myself why I was there and took a few seconds to take in the faces of the audience. Their eyes were filled with great admiration for Colonel North. Sensing a responsibility to express the same shared feelings as everyone, I took a deep breath and called upon my heart to occupy my mind.

"Colonel Oliver North, I am in awe and humbled that I stand before you on behalf of an incredible group of people, 'Support Our War Heroes'—and especially our heroes tonight . . . with an opportunity to present to you something I created with my God-given talent. I never dreamed of such an opportunity.

"I would like to ask you a question," I said, turning toward him. "When you were a young man, would you have ever thought that you would be a historic hero in America?"

With a slight humble tilt of his head downward, he shook his head no.

I continued, "Great things and large responsibilities were destined for you, all of which you accepted because greatness has been placed upon your heart for your country.

"In your life you have been in a position to be an example to millions of Americans, and tonight to hundreds, but more importantly, to the heroes that are here in this room. Between you and these heroes there is the exchange of a language that is shared in a glance, a nod, a salute, and a handshake. A language that is rich in unity, camaraderie, appreciation, and hope.

"In this life some are asked to make greater sacrifices in order to see their hope fulfilled. Sometimes hope and sacrifice are inseparable. Without hope there is no leadership. Without hope there is no gain. Without hope there can be no fulfillment."

Periodically I glanced up at him, and at one point, I saw something. Within his eyes seemed to be a hero's tear, glossed over with gratitude. Trying to keep my focus, I returned to my paper, but in the back of my mind, I thought of his humble expression, which confirmed every great thought we had of him.

"So tonight, this moment in time, hope is fulfilled, hope is gained, and hope is acknowledged by the great leadership in this room.

"It is our hope that you accept and wear this pin as a reminder of the unspoken language you share with the heroes and families who serve this country. The presentation of the 'Star of Hope™' is from all of us, and is given to you in recognition of your continued, exemplary leadership and service to our country.

"You are a real American hero! Thank you."

Rising to their feet with cheers and whistles, the guests applauded in a standing ovation.

I saw my hands shaking as I raised the beautifully polished Star of Hope pin to Colonel Oliver North's lapel. I looked at my hands as if they belonged to someone else. The magnitude of who this hero was had hit me; it was nerve-shaking and at the same time, extremely gratifying. Unbeknownst to anyone around, I was having trouble getting the pin through the fabric of his jacket.

In a low and confident voice, he said, "Just push it through."

At the end of the event, Colonel North said to me, "You have a gift." Wanting to know if he liked the pin and what he thought of the presentation, I couldn't help but ask, "What might that be?"

Pausing, he turned, facing me straight on, and then stepped forward into my comfort zone—I guess it was a military thing. Because of his assertive body language, thoughts of humility ran through my mind, as to say, "How dare you fish for compliments when we have real heroes here tonight?" Instead, with a pleasant but sincere expression, he looked me in the eyes and said, "In the book of Romans, Saint Paul writes about hope. He did no better job than you did here tonight."

I was speechless. I must have floated a few feet off the ground. Obviously I am no comparison to Saint Paul, but it was one of the highest compliments I would receive in my life and will never be forgotten.

Retired Lieutenant Colonel Oliver North

Admiring the soldiers that night inspired me to continue to share my love for America the only way I know how: jewelry designs. Hope is freedom, and it is the inspiration for some of the greatest American achievements. Hope lies within the American Dream. That hope began with the guardians of our nation, the Founding Fathers, so that "We The People" govern our own abilities toward life, liberty and the pursuit of happiness as Americans.

CHAPTER 18
America

Where Dreams are Achieved

Statue of Liberty

Amer(A)merica is the icon of possibility. Growing up, I was taught at home and in elementary school to always respect and appreciate my country. Proudly, every classroom displayed both the flag and the U.S. presidents. As little people in school, we faced the American flag, and with our hands over our hearts, we pledged allegiance to our country every day. Then we would sing "My Country 'Tis of Thee . . ." Through a child's eyes, these events and images brought about a desire to pursue the

American Dream. Seeing the pictures of our presidents reminded us that at one time, they were kids too, just like us, and they too dreamt about what they wanted to be when they grew up. But we were also taught that you had to work for America's golden opportunities, you were entitled to nothing, and that success was up to each one of us. We were taught that hard work towards our goals had a value in and of itself.

Inexplicable changes began to occur. I don't know exactly when and how it happened, but we stopped singing "My Country, 'Tis of Thee" in school and the images of the presidents were only to be seen in history books. But I never stopped that song in my heart or lost sight of those inspiring images. I believe in the American Dream, just as my ancestors and grandparents did.

Even though I never met my grandparents, I credit them for my patriotism. Each time their stories were shared by a member of the family, I fell in love with America even more. They believed that with hard work and perseverance, anything is possible in this country, and that each person's American Dream is unique to them.

With this philosophy in mind, I began to create patriotic jewelry. The designs commemorated the road traveled by so many of our ancestors and the fact that the American Dream is still obtainable today.

Sketch and Finished Pendant: Lady Liberty Jewelry Design by Anne Dale

By coincidence my Lady Liberty pendant was completed just in time for the 125th anniversary of the Statue of Liberty in 2011. I recall the evening I completed the design: I locked the door to the jewelry store behind the last customer for the day. All the lights were out except for the brightest one that was stationed over my workbench. There she patiently waited for me to continue echoing her message to the world. My jeweler's file shaped her to the perfection that my skill would allow. She will be worth more than green paper to some, more than beauty to others. She holds value to thousands of those who seek her. Although Lady Liberty is 125 years old, her strength and willingness to offer opportunity make her timeless. As I finished my work, I was filled with wonder and appreciation. I reflected on the boldness of my grandfather who left his country to come to America at the age of sixteen. My mother's father, who was a customs inspector in New York, worked periodic shifts on Ellis Island after World War II. My mother told stories of how he sympathetically witnessed the pain-stricken faces of many Jewish immigrants as Lady Liberty welcomed them to America. My ancestors led me to this moment in my life.

Anne's grandfather Francis Allen (front row, second from right)
with fellow customs officers

It was time for me to clean up the shop. Grabbing a broom to sweep up the floor, my mind was flooded with memories of the blind broom man, and his strong and admirable desire to remain self-sufficient. Although blind, he still pursued his own American Dream. He believed that she, the iconic image of America and all that she represented, offered opportunity for him, not in spite of his disability, but for his abilities.

Thirty years after my first visit to the Statue of Liberty, I would go back while on a business trip. Initially, I walked the perimeter of her skirting gown, studying her poise and wondering if she had changed. Did she age as I did? Her sandal strap was untied, exemplifying an eagerness to show the world her leadership as she stepped forward leading the way. But now I viewed Lady Liberty with the eyes of a wife, mother, business owner, and entrepreneur. Years ago, I didn't recall such intriguing details. She was even more magnificent than I remembered.

Every detail of "Liberty Enlightening the World" represents a symbol of freedom and enlightenment. In her crown, the twenty-five windows depict the natural minerals of the earth, and the seven spikes of the crown portray the seven continents; her torch symbolizes enlightenment, and underfoot liberty is crushing the chains of slavery. She firmly holds in her left hand a tablet with the inscription "July 4, 1776," the day of America's independence from Britain. As the sun rises and sets on her, it is said she can appear different with each passing day. Perhaps it is Lady Liberty's way of letting us know she is alive for every generation.

Taking it all in, I sat on a park bench watching the many visitors. My fascination with her led to many thoughts. As Americans, some of our ancestors came from afar. Some sailed through New York's harbor, having crossed the mighty Atlantic Ocean with a hopeful heart. As a beacon of light for those to find their way, she would, for some, be their first vision and impression of America. Between the years of 1892 and 1954, immigrants were required to disembark at Lady Liberty's neighboring island, Ellis Island. Upon their arrival, those hoping for citizenship were suspended between fear and hope in a new world. Ellis Island would receive 12 million people, and each person had to be vetted by a customs inspector. The inspectors' prime task was to question new arrivals, verify their documented information from the manifest, and evaluate the state of their health. Some inspectors would assess an immigrant's health by watching how well he or she could climb the stairs of the baggage area to the Great Hall. With chalk, the inspectors marked the clothing of immigrants who required further medical evaluation: "E" for eyes, "H" for Heart, "S" for senility, and so on. According to a 1917 U.S. Public Health Service manual, nine out of 100 immigrants were marked with an "X" for mental disease. Twenty percent of all immigrants were detained for inspection, some being held for days or even weeks on the island.

During my return visit, I was invited by a National Park Ranger to tour a historic part of Ellis Island that had been closed to the public since 1950. The area had been used for detainees and included the medical facility, psychiatric ward, and morgue. It was an eerie place that had processed thousands of people in their quest for the America Dream.

With January's temperatures and cold winds coming off the Atlantic waves, the tour was frigid. Even while being wrapped in my coat, gloves, and scarf, the only warmth was the breath I exhaled. The tour began with quiet, vacant buildings that had empty, dismal, gray-colored rooms, but I knew the walls had witnessed history, absorbing stories of fear, hope, and tears. Because the building had no electricity and no other tourists were around, the excursion took on a haunting, yet contemplative feel. Preoccupied with my thoughts, the cold made me more sympathetic toward the ghostly immigrants who remained in my mind. The afternoon sun that shone through the broken window panes projected a small amount of light for the many dark shadows that occupied corners upon every turn. As I walked, the sound of my heels echoed in the distance down a long, creepy, and barren hall. Most immigrants who walked down these hallways likely knew that their American Dream could end here. It must have been terrifying. These were the foyers that led to the hospital where they were treated for illness or psychological evaluation. Standing inside the small, concrete, and cell-like units, I tried to imagine how it must have been for those who traveled so far, only to be denied entrance into the United States. Perhaps not intentionally, the architectural layout of some of the wards tormented patients with a beautiful window view of Lady Liberty standing gloriously in the harbor. Those whose health improved were allowed to enter America; others would be deported. Some remained on the Island until their death. Twenty thousand adults and fourteen thousand children perished on Ellis Island. Their hopes turned into sorrow and tragedy.

Millions of others left their homes in foreign lands and were offered the chance for a new way of life. Most arrived with nothing but a suitcase, others with just the clothes on their backs. But they brought with them an enormous amount of hope for the opportunity of a better life—the American Dream. Their journey alone compelled me to rethink the way I defined success. I realized that success can be equated to a person's ambition, drive, sacrifice, and hard work, even if in the end their ultimate American Dream was not personally realized. As we persevere in the journey toward our goals, we gauge our success. For the immigrants, their voyage of hope to America was their success.

After an incredible and emotional day visiting the two islands, I headed back to my hotel. Burning brightly in my mind was the memory of the wish that I had made thirty years ago at the age of seventeen when I had peered through the windows of the Statue of Liberty's crown. My wish had taken root, but not without the hopes and sacrifices of many ancestors.

Riding on the subway into the city, I glanced at the passengers whose bloodlines mirrored the multicultural faces of their ancestors who gave to them their chance to pursue the American Dream. Unable to shake the image of the ghostly immigrants, I was unsettled by the passengers' faces that suggested a discontentment with life. I wondered if they pursued opportunity and believed in possibilities, or had they become complacent for whatever life handed them? This was not at all what the immigrants of the nineteenth and early twentieth centuries were made of. As I swayed with the movement of the train, I thought of patriotic people—Corporal Matthew Cole, Colonel Oliver North, the soldiers, my grandparents, even my school teachers. Lady Liberty now present in my head and on my heart, echoed the word "opportunity."

View of the Statue of Liberty from the infirmary on Ellis Island

Months later, I would again return to the Statue of Liberty and Ellis Island to knock on the golden door of opportunity. I would present my patriotic designs of jewelry for the Liberty Island Gift Store with the hope that they would buy the collection for their shop. A dream come true, now available on the Island is a segment of the collection, and I am humbly honored for this privilege that has been bestowed upon me: to use the talent God gave to me to represent America to all who visit Lady Liberty.

CHAPTER 19

LaPearlite®

Power of One

Anne Mining for LaPearlite®

I was happy believing that my career was satisfying and complete. That was until one day something extraordinary happened, something beyond my wildest dreams, a discovery that could be defined as an American Dream for a gemologist. I had stumbled upon an amazing treasure; I discovered a gemstone. It was a new gemstone that had hidden itself from the world for hundreds of thousands of years, waiting for the right moment to reveal itself. And much like the shepherd in my story to Ms. Laurent, I also am humbled that it has entrusted me to discover and introduce it to the jewelry industry. With few other gemstones mined for fine jewelry in the United States, this new discovery presents a golden opportunity.

Every year, I attend the largest gem show in the world with the same enthusiasm as when I was a child. My lucky stone still travels with me, and my eyes still widen with the wonderment of seeing the spectacular display of gems shining in the bright lights. I now understand the clamor of excited voices and the many questions related to gemology. I am no longer timid; I am the grown-up at the gem show, having fulfilled my dream to become a gemologist. But the 2011 gem show in particular would be unlike any other because I was traveling with something very special that no human eye—not even those of professionals in the gem industry—had ever seen: the newly discovered gemstone. As I told its story and shared its beauty, I watched gem enthusiasts become amazed just as I was. Question after question was asked, such as, "How did you discover it?" "Is it plentiful?" and "What's its predicted value?"

The discovery of this new gemstone coincides with a storm of life that would affect America's dependency on the Gulf of Mexico, the 2010 BP/Deep Water Horizon oil spill. As a native of Louisiana, I value the Gulf Coast's natural resources. Besides its pristine waters that provide delicious seafood and endless opportunities for recreation, economically, the Gulf is the largest oil producing region in the U.S. Indeed, the Gulf of Mexico is hugely important to both Louisiana and the country as a whole; it really is "America's Gulf."

The broadcasted television images of oil spewing into the Gulf of Mexico after the explosion of a drilling rig brought only consternation. Monstrous oil blobs began to tarnish the beaches of the Gulf Coast states and marred public perception of the Gulf's seafood industry. Media reports forecasted concern with regard to seafood production. Those restless thoughts heightened my desire to help those affected, so I went out and spent four hundred dollars on seafood to freeze for the upcoming holidays. I sat in the evening sun, shucking oysters and drinking a cold beer. All at once my eyes were captivated with how the sun's golden rays happened to fall upon an area deep inside one of the shells I was holding. It glistened in a brilliant way, highlighting unique gem-like characteristics. Intrigued by its gemological appeal, I studied it, pondering its beauty and potential. My gemologist brain raced with thoughts; it was unlike any gem I had ever seen. I wondered why no one had ever discovered this. Examining it further, I tried to categorize it, but it was different from pearls or Mother of Pearl; it almost looked opal-ish. It was an inconceivable moment of discovery. Excitedly, I stood up and called for Mike: "Look at this!" As I described its mesmerizing beauty, the name "LaPearlite" naturally fell from my lips, and so it would be called.

Mike and I quickly set out to cut and polish that unique area of the oyster's bivalve. As we did, it came to life even more. We saw more beauty unfold, golden rings and swirls, some displaying magical underlying layers of sheen, as if it reflected the scenic waters it came from. We knew its long-awaited beauty was in our hands to share with others. In our research and development, we realized that with each gemstone we cut, we unveiled even more appealing individual characteristics. We also realized this discovery was bigger than us—it was meant to be. "Oyster mining" became a new term in my vocabulary and a new important activity for me.

LaPearlite is derived from one of the most important oysters to the U.S., the *Crassostrea virginica* mollusk. This mollusk is predominantly found in the Gulf of Mexico, mainly in the brackish, coastal waters of Louisiana that support a variety of elements and minerals, all of which contribute to the gemstone's uniqueness. Although the mollusk does not produce fine pearls, it respectfully possesses another natural beauty valued by the gem and jewelry trade. LaPearlite occurs in a rare area of the oyster's bivalve capable of producing a beautiful, symmetrical cabochon cut gemstone. This occurs in only approximately 8 percent of these oysters. To put it into perspective by comparing it with diamonds within the industry, only 20 percent of all diamonds mined actually make it into a jewelry store.

Feeling a responsibility as the gem's guardian, I knew LaPearl-ite was to go beyond the front doors of my retail jewelry store. Since it represented the beauty and value of both America's Gulf and Louisiana's waterways, I went to the state legislature to propose a bill to make it the official Louisiana state gemstone. When Bill 246 was presented to both the House and Senate Committees, I was given the opportunity to speak on its behalf. My unfamiliarity with legislative protocol and procedure made for an intimidating experience. I sat at a small table and chair that was positioned below an elevated tier of politicians. Leaning forward to reach the table that was in front of me, I tried to discreetly scoot in the heavy metal chair that seemed anchored, while at the same time I adjusted the long, thin, sound-sensitive microphone that shrieked with each of my movements. My inexperience was obvious. I ended up sitting on the edge of my seat; metaphorically, it summed up my nervousness.

The legislative committee requested to see samples of the gemstones. As a tray of LaPearlite gemstones was passed around, I emphasized its potential. Legislators seemed intrigued by not only its discovery, but also its beauty. For Louisianians, the oyster shell has been around forever. Images of oysters in dumpsters and driveways were etched in everyone's mind. Legislators sought answers as to why its bivalve all of the sudden revealed a hidden beauty that had value to the state. For legislators to accept and understand why no one in the past had discovered this gem, certain questions needed to be answered. Their questions were different from those of gem enthusiasts, but as a teacher of gemology, they were fairly easy to answer.

"What constitutes a gem?" was one of the questions.

"The Federal Trade Commission's regulations require four criteria—beauty, rarity, durability, and symmetry . . . this gemstone possesses all four."

It was obviously beautiful. Not all Crassostrea mollusks could produce this beautiful gem, thus making them rare. It was soft but durable, able to be worn and adorned in jewelry such as pendants and earrings. The stone's durability on Moh's hardness scale is similar to other gems such as pearls, opals, and turquoise. The cabochon cut, referring to its domed top and flat bottom, offered symmetrical balance, thus disqualifying any odd polished shapes or tablets that might be cut randomly for cheap inlays. The achieved style of cabochon cut fulfilled the Federal Trade Commission's requirement of symmetry, thereby sustaining the integrity and value of the gemstone.

Gold, custom-made LaPearlite necklaces

Representative Scott Simon, Anne Dale, and Ewell Smith, Executive Director of the Louisiana Seafood Promotion and Marketing Board

In the midst of questions and answers, the author of the bill, Representative Scott Simon, held up an acknowledgment that I had received from the Smithsonian Institute which confirmed that LaPerlite was nationally recognized as gemstone. House Bill 246 would pass, making the Cabochon Cut derived from the *Crassostrea viriginca* mollusk the Louisiana state gemstone. The bill was officially signed by Governor Bobby Jindal and became law on August 15, 2011.

Smithsonian Institution
NATIONAL MUSEUM OF NATURAL HISTORY

Certificate of Appreciation

awarded to

Anne Dale

In recognition of the generous gift of LaPearlite to the

United States National Gem Collection

Certificate from the Smithsonian Museum of Natural History recognizing LaPearlite

American Dreams are alive in this generation; I discovered the Louisiana State Gemstone. Dreams begin with one idea at a time —the power of one.

CHAPTER 20

Blind Eyes Discover

Live Life From the Inside Out

Lawrence Schlaudecker, circa 1900

My one-block universe as a child traveled the borders of my imagination. Still today I journey to wonderful places, experience new opportunities, and learn to embrace the love of friends and family. But whether I travel as a gemologist, a jeweler, or an entrepreneur, I carry with me the people who've influenced my life, especially one individual who helped guide me down a path to success—the blind broom man. He exemplified perseverance and determination. His optimism inspired me and demonstrated the value of hard work. He taught me how to listen to the call of opportunity. He was a mentor whose life and name had always been a mystery—that is until one day, forty some years later. August of 2012, the week Hurricane Isaac loomed in the Gulf, the blind broom man astonishingly reappeared in my life. It was as if he blew in with the winds of Isaac. His return also uniquely coincided with the writing of what I thought was to be the last chapter of this book, "LaPearlite®."

Walking back into my life, his return was by no means a coincidence. It began over a casual conversation between two friends at the neighboring hairdresser's shop, both of whom are avid readers and often discuss books. I had previously shared my manuscript with one of the ladies.

"Did you know Anne Dale is writing a book?" the friend asked the hairdresser.

"Really? What's the book about?" she asked.

As the client described the topic of my manuscript, she mentioned, "Well there is this blind broom man who went around selling brooms in her neighborhood when she was a little girl."

The hairdresser, who was listening interrupted, immediately inquiring as to the neighborhood I grew up in. By chance, an incredible coincidence was realized.

"That was my great uncle!" she exclaimed.

Amazed by the revelation, the friend quickly drove over to the jewelry store to share the news. She ran into the store, gasping for air, and shouted, "I know the name of the blind man who sold the brooms to your mom when you were a kid!"

Confused, I asked, "What?"

Convinced, she declared, "The name of the blind man was Lawrence Schlaudecker!"

In disbelief, I asked, "How do you know this?"

I was astounded as she began to share his background. My friend could see the dazed look on my face as I tried to process the odds of this.

My friend added, "How many blind men sold brooms in your neighborhood?"

Acknowledging her point, I answered, "Only one."

The grace of truth fell upon me. Validating this discovery, I called out questions as fast as I could. Raising my arm to indicate height, I asked, "Was her great uncle this tall? What about his

Adam's apple? Was it large? Did he wear dark glasses? Do you have a picture of him?"

Question after question, she confirmed the blind man's identity. Overwhelmed, tears streamed down my face. Just twenty-four hours earlier I was "knocking," asking for the answer to a prayer. Wanting to satisfy my curiosity and know who the blind broom man really was, I asked God to reveal his life. Stunned by my friend's revelation, I became weak; my legs felt like rubber, I needed to sit down. Everything in my busy little world in the jewelry store had just stopped; it was a joyous epiphany. Here I was, now a grown woman, married with children, and the blind man had really returned. But this time it would be the blind man's door that opened, allowing me to see into his life. Embracing his return, I began researching archives and meeting with the very few people left alive who actually knew something about him. I found myself revisiting memories that had grown hazy through the years. It was as if he said, "Tell my story, Anne. Tell my story and reveal the 'gift' I gave to you so long ago."

— § —

Mr. Schlaudecker was born in New Orleans in 1892 to parents of German descent. He was one of seven brothers, all of whom were robust and handsome men. Being part of a large family, his help was always needed; even at the age of five, he shared in family chores. Like me, he too was raised to understand that his siblings were his responsibility. By age thirteen, he was employed as a tinsmith, proudly contributing his earnings to the family just as his brothers did. Indeed, the men of the house were expected to support the family with a portion of the wages they earned.

One day, while working alongside a coworker who was soldering iron, a flame flew into Lawrence's left eye, scorching it and leaving him with one functioning eye. With his restricted vision he would quickly have to learn how to become more reliant on his instincts and senses. As a young teen, he coped with his disability as best he could, relying on personal fortitude as well as the guidance of his parents. They taught him from an early age that self-pity had no place in the Schlaudeckers' household. They knew that allowing him to feel sorry for himself might cripple him psychologically for the rest of his life. With a determined attitude and a supportive family, Lawrence refused to allow his injury to define himself or his abilities. He had learned from his father and brothers that skill in a trade possessed value; it meant being employed, and employment demonstrated self-worth. As he continued sharing in the family workload, he explored a variety of trades.

Lawrence Schlaudecker, December 23, 1892–December 12, 1988

He gravitated toward jobs that allowed him the independence to work on his own—like me, he loved the prospect of being self-employed, depending on no one but himself. His patience and creative side relished in repairing, restoring, and painting furniture and houses, all of which he seemed to possess a natural talent for. His abilities and reputation as an excellent craftsman were sought after, keeping him busy and gainfully employed as he moved from one jobsite to another, city to city. His motivation was not money, but dignity, independence, and ambition. He took pride in his work. His character, outwardly masculine and unrelenting, could also be warm and charitable, as he freely shared his earnings with those less fortunate.

Soon his "me" turned to "we" when he accepted a job in Amite, Louisiana. While living in a boarding home near a jobsite, he would meet the love of his life, the daughter of his French immigrant landlord, Elizabeth Palmier. He and Elizabeth courted, and soon he referred to her as his "Lillie." Because Amite was a small town, employment was scarce, but he didn't want to leave his Lille. He never lost his faith or confidence in his abilities. Taking courage in God's provocation, he knew their needs could be met by his willingness and his good work ethic. Lillie was the one for him. Following his heart, on New Year's Eve in 1916, he and Lillie married. Wanting to make their wedding day special, he spent the only money he had in his pocket, sixty-five cents, on dinner and fireworks. By the standards of the day, he had spent a fairly sizeable sum to give his new bride a memorable wedding day.

In 1920 he was commissioned to paint and refurbish a church in a nearby town. While he was building a scaffold to reach the church's high ceilings, tragedy struck him once again. As he hammered an old nail, a piece broke off and lodged into his only seeing eye. He was blinded instantly; darkness fell all around him. At twenty-eight years old, he lay blind in a hospital in New Orleans. Medical experts, at a loss for how to restore his sight, attempted to use a powerful magnet to remove the piece of nail, but the procedure only made it worse. The magnet pulled the jagged nail shard across his eye, severing many of the blood vessels, ultimately requiring removal of the eye altogether.

Attempting to face his demons, he wrestled not to keep company with despair. Calling on the Lord, he held onto his faith with courage and conviction. For ten days after his accident, he pondered and prayed while recovering, and on the tenth day there was a knock on his hospital door. It was a stranger, a humanitarian, who told him about a new concept, a rehabilitation program at the Light House for the Blind in New Orleans. The Light House taught a trade in making brooms, products that the blind could sell door to door. He felt it was an answer to his prayer and accepted the knock of opportunity. Determined to reclaim his dignity, within three months, he mastered the skill of making brooms both by hand and with the use of a large industrial, mass-producing machine that the Light House had purchased. He would be one of the first to graduate from the Light House for the Blind's occupational program. Since he had mastered both techniques of craftsmanship, the Light House had hoped that he would stay on and instruct others, but his heart knew his home was wherever Lillie wanted to be, which Amite was.

With his grit and his determination, he began selling brooms door to door. However, ambitious in his desire to be productive and self-sufficient, Lawrence had greater aspirations. He wanted to start his own business, manufacturing both brooms and mops on a much broader scale to supply both households and businesses. In order to achieve his goal, he would need to acquire the same mass-producing broom machine he had mastered while at the Light House for the Blind. However, the investment would require additional money that he didn't have. He would also need a place to operate such an expansive means of production. Confident and never accepting defeat, he borrowed money to fund his dream. Refusing handouts, he vowed to pay back every dime. He rented a neighbor's garage, which he eventually owned, and he paid back his loans with interest and established his business, Schlaudecker's Brooms & Mops.

Since Amite was a quaint and friendly town, people often stopped by to watch him make his brooms. It was nerve-wracking for the onlookers to observe him operate his noisy, sizable, and dangerous machinery. It had razor-sharp blades and large sewing needles that passed just inches from his hands. He had to learn every detail of his equipment in order to operate and repair it himself. Believing safety to be paramount, he took numerous safety precautions and fashioned his own protective equipment. He was proud to own one of the few electric binding broom machines of its kind in the country, a sentiment that came through in an interview with the *Daily Star* in Hammond, Louisiana.

"I enjoy my work," he said. "It keeps me fit. One machine requires work with my feet and that helps keep me in shape."

Initially, he delivered his brooms and mops in a wheel barrel. But as his business expanded, the increased number of deliveries required that he find a more efficient method that would allow him to get his products to customers. Blind, he purchased his first automobile, a Chevrolet. Lillie served as the designated driver, bringing him from one location to another and traveling to neighboring cities, hospitals, and to a total of fifty-two schools. Possessing a good business sense, he bartered when his sales were lean, swapping his brooms for other products: chickens, eggs, sweet potatoes, gasoline. There were endless possibilities for a sharp mind like his.

Regarded as a role model in his community, Mr. Schlaudecker was elected to public office as Justice of the Peace. While managing his busy broom business, he held the elected office for twenty straight years from 1940 to 1960. As a blind Justice of the Peace— the scales of fairness could not be more balanced than that! Lacking sight, his judgment could dismiss race, appearance, wealth, or poverty but not the presented facts of right or wrong. During hearings, there were times he had to be quick on his feet, boldly having to stop feuds that escalated into physical altercations. Sometimes he had to throw a punch into the empty air in order to defend himself. One of the most treasured joys of his elected position was uniting couples in matrimony.

His business prospered, and throughout the years, he continued to listen to people and grow in wisdom. Drawing his strength from the Lord, he attributed his bestowed blessings to God's infinite love. He was interviewed by the *Daily Star's* "Fun Guide" at the age of eighty-three, saying, "I have worked all my life. I never used my blindness for sympathy or charity. I know it's God and God alone that has helped me take care of my burden. I went blind, but I didn't stay blind."

He and Lillie had no children, but together they affectionately embraced friends as extended family. Darkness would fall upon him once again, but this time it was in his heart. Lillie passed away. She was his business partner, his earthly eyes, but more so, his soul mate.

Lawrence and Elizabeth "Lillie" Schlaudecker
posing in front of their Chevrolet.

Nearing the age of ninety-five, Mr. Schlaudecker's health began to decline. Needing physical assistance, he made the decision to enter a state nursing home but was refused because his assets exceeded the state's entry requirements. Since money was never his motive in life, it made it easy for him to sell everything he owned—his house, car, and even his once prized broom-making machine. The rumor was that after he sold everything, he went around town and gave his money to every church in the community.

In 1988, twelve days before his ninety-sixth birthday, he died. Engraved on his tombstone is a biblical verse he lived by, "Waiting for the Lord with courage" from Psalms 27:14.

On August 28, 2012, the eve of the anniversary of Hurricane Katrina, I needed courage as I heard the news reports on Hurricane Isaac's impending approach. Preparations were made into the evening. Isaac was classified as a category one hurricane with expected winds of 80 to 100 mph, as well as storm surges and wide spread power outages. Realizing that the changing winds could happen once again, anxiety occupied my mind. To soothe my nerves, I reclined in a living room chair. Slowly I breathed in and out, and a memory came back to me.

The Gift

I recall a time when my mother left me at the door with Mr. Schlaudecker. Quietly, I stood in front of him, gazing curiously as I always did. Slightly curving the palm of his hand upward, he slowly extended it out toward me. I was confused and wondered if he thought I would hand him mama's money? Was he expecting a meet-and-greet like the grown-ups? Perhaps he was holding something for me to see? With his hand just above the level of my eyes, I stood up on my toes and peered over. I saw nothing but his callused hand and the shank of his magic ring which later he would have to sell. Believing him to be magical, I thought that it must be a trick he wanted to show me, so I stared into his palm, waiting. As I exhaled, my breath landed in his palm; suddenly snatching it, he quickly closed his hand tightly. Keeping it, he securely placed my breath in the top pocket of his shirt. He smiled and gently patted his pocket, as if the captured breath belonged to him.

"Thank you," he said.

Even though I was taken by surprise, I thought this was funny. With a little girl's chuckle, I smiled back.

He told me, "Remember, not everything valuable is visible. Learn to see what your eyes can't, but what your heart can."

He made the invisible visible for me. His words of wisdom have never left me, nor have I ever forgotten him.

Now that time had passed, I realized that if given the chance, I would share with him one of my gifts, something that once connected our first encounter. Wishing, I beckoned him once more with the eyes of my heart to the door of my mind. In my imagination, I could see him standing upright, strong, and wearing his coppola.

"Hello, Mr. Lawrence John Schlaudecker!"

Taking a rest from the weight of the brooms, I could practically see him slide the bundle off of his shoulder. "Hello, Mrs. Anne Dale!"

Overwhelmed by wanting to say so much to him, I attempted to express my gratitude. "Thank you for being an inspiration. Your life is an example of courage and optimism."

With a humble smile, he replied, "My vision relies on attitude and I listen for opportunity. I had to learn to see from within."

"I have a gift for you. I made it myself."

Invitingly, he responded, "Really?"

Removing a LaPearlite gemstone ring from my finger, I reached for his calloused hand and replaced the ring he had to sell all those years ago. He felt the ring's detail, identifying and appreciating the craftsmanship. He studied it, feeling the unique coolness and smoothness of the newly discovered LaPearlite gemstone. He closed his hand, bending his wrist about, recalling a familiar comfort he once felt so long ago. Our worlds collided.

Grateful, he responded, "Thank you."

I too was delighted, seeing how nice the ring looked on his strong hand and knowing it was appreciated. I watched the ring flicker in the sun as he picked up the brooms to rest them on his shoulder.

Tipping me farewell with his cap, he started to walk away.

Uncertain if he would ever return, I called out, "Hey, wait. What's next?"

Turning back toward me, his confident voice projected, "Live from the inside out, and opportunity will find you."

Feeling smitten about our imaginary encounter, I thought about my destiny that life's storms created. However, the silence of my aloneness ended abruptly with the sound of an explosion in the neighborhood. A power transformer blew, and the lights went out. In the darkness I sat. I felt the light of the blind broom man's courage as I waited for the voice of opportunity, and once again, I was swept away.

About the Author

Anne Dale, a professional gemologist and jewelry designer, is a native of Louisiana.

She is the founder of "Jeweler For a Cause®" and "Jewelry For a Cause®." After Hurricane Katrina, she created the "I Know What it Means to Love New Orleans®" jewelry design which raised over a quarter of a million dollars for storm victims.

In 2010, Anne discovered the Louisiana state gemstone, the cabochon cut derived from the Crassostrea virginica mollusk, also known as LaPearlite.

Anne is a speaker, author, educator, entrepreneur, and philanthropist.

Anne is a Graduate Gemologist of the Gemological Institute of America, Professional Gemologist of the Columbia School of Gemology, and a Lifetime Fellow of the Gemmological Association of Great Britain.

She has assisted in establishing gemological courses in colleges and trade schools, and she serves as an expert witness for the Internal Revenue Service. Anne is a public speaker and radio show host.

Anne is a recipient of the Louisiana Artist Award, the Diamond in the Rough Award by the Association of Women Gemologists, and the Woman of the Year Award by the Professional Business Women's Association of Saint Tammany Parish, Louisiana.

She is married to Michael Dale, a master jeweler and her business partner, of Anne Dale Jeweler, LLC, in Mandeville, Louisiana.